LOCAL INITIATIVES FOR JOB CREATION

ENTERPRISING WOMEN

ORGANISATION FOR ECONOMIC CO-OPERATION AND DEVELOPMENT

Pursuant to article 1 of the Convention signed in Paris on 14th December 1960, and which came into force on 30th September 1961, the Organisation for Economic Co-operation and Development (OECD) shall promote policies designed:

- to achieve the highest sustainable economic growth and employment and a rising standard of living in Member countries, while maintaining financial stability, and thus to contribute to the development of the world economy;
- to contribute to sound economic expansion in Member as well as non-member countries in the process of economic development; and
- to contribute to the expansion of world trade on a multilateral, non-discriminatory basis in accordance with international obligations.

The original Member countries of the OECD are Austria, Belgium, Canada, Denmark, France, the Federal Republic of Germany, Greece, Iceland, Ireland, Italy, Luxembourg, the Netherlands, Norway, Portugal, Spain, Sweden, Switzerland, Turkey, the United Kingdom and the United States. The following countries became Members subsequently through accession at the dates indicated hereafter: Japan (28th April 1964), Finland (28th January 1969), Australia (7th June 1971) and New Zealand (29th May 1973).

The Socialist Federal Republic of Yugoslavia takes part in some of the work of the OECD (agreement of 28th October 1961).

Publié en français sous le titre:

INITIATIVES LOCALES DE CRÉATION D'EMPLOIS :
ENTREPRENDRE AU FÉMININ

Reprinted, 1992

PREFACE

In the United States, a third of business owners are women; their numbers are increasing one-and-a-half times faster than men, and it is expected that by the year 2000 one American business leader in two will be female. Roughly the same proportion can be found in the Federal Republic of Germany, Canada and France, at least as regards owners of new firms.

The 1980s have therefore been a period of rapid growth of self-employment and business creation by women. Yet this trend towards a search for greater economic independence should not obscure the fact that women still suffer from discrimination and women's jobs still tend to be more precarious than men's.

This growth of female entrepreneurship is part of a more general expansion of innovation and business creation, resulting in new kinds of people becoming business leaders and contributing to the gradual restructuring of local economies.

This study is based on the proceedings of a Conference on Women — Local Initiatives — Job Creation, which took place in Oslo in 1987, together with information collected in participating countries on developments since then. It not only describes and analyses the progress already made, but draws the attention of public authorities and the business community to the need to expand female entrepreneurship by encouraging women to set up new businesses, making it easier for them to become self-employed, and being more considerate of women's wishes and potential in this area. The report highlights the particular roles of all those involved and offers broad guidelines for the types of action that should be encouraged in the future in the pursuit of greater fairness and efficiency.

ALSO AVAILABLE

Evaluating Labour Market and Social Programmes. The State of a Complex Art (1991)
(81 91 01 1) ISBN 92-64-13537-5   FF155   £20.00   US$37.00   DM60

Local Initiatives for Employment Creation
Implementing Change. Entrepreneurship and Local Initiative (1990)
(84 90 01 1) ISBN 92-64-13360-7   FF70   £8.50   US$15.00   DM27

OECD Employment Outlook
1991 (1991)
(81 91 02 1) ISBN 92-64-13540-5   FF200   £26.00   US$48.00   DM78

OECD Social Policy Studies
No. 8 – Lone-Parent Families: The Economic Challenge (1990)
(81 89 04 1) ISBN 92-64-13303-8   FF160   £20.00   US$34.00   DM66

Prices charged at the OECD Bookshop.

*THE OECD CATALOGUE OF PUBLICATIONS and supplements will be sent free of charge
on request addressed either to OECD Publications Service,
or to the OECD Distributor in your country.*

ABOUT THE AUTHORS

Candida G. Brush (author of chapter III) is a research assistant and doctoral student at Boston University and the author of several publications related to women's business development.

Sara K. Gould (co-editor of the book and co-author of chapter VI) is the director of the Economic Development Project of the Ms. Foundation for Women and works extensively on programme and strategic planning with grassroots women's organisations undertaking economic development projects across the U.S.

Kathryn Keeley (author of chapter V) is co-founder and president of Women's Economic Development Corporation (WEDCO), a women's organisation located in St. Paul, Minnesota, whose mission is to secure a stronger economic future for women through business development.

Julianne Malveaux, Ph.D. (author of chapter II) is a San Francisco-based economist and writer and research associate at the Institute of Industrial Relations at the University of California, Berkeley.

Julia Parzen (co-editor of the book and co-author of chapter VI), a co-founder of Working Assets Money Fund, is an author, teacher, consultant, and entrepreneur in the field of development banking and social investment based in Chicago, Illinois.

Beth Siegel (author of chapter I) is a partner in Mt. Auburn Associates, an economic development consulting firm based in Somerville, Massachusetts.

Chris Weiss (author of chapter IV) is an economic development practitioner based in West Virginia and is on the staff of both the Ms. Foundation for Women and Women's World Banking.

TABLE OF CONTENTS

Part I

SETTING THE SCENE

Part II

LOCAL RESPONSES: WHAT IS AND WHAT COULD BE

Part I

SETTING THE SCENE

The growing interest among OECD Member countries in enterprise creation programmes aimed at women results from the interaction of three important forces which have evolved over time. First, an increasing number of practitioners and policymakers are validating enterprise creation strategies as an integral part of local economic development plans. Second, the role of women in the labour force has dramatically expanded. Women now appear in every role and occupation, including the role of entrepreneur. Finally, policymakers are recognising that women, particularly low-income and minority women, face unique barriers to achieving their entrepreneurial potential.

The chapters of Part I examine these forces in depth, discuss their effect on women's choice of self-employment, and offer insights into how they can be harnessed to shape successful entrepreneurship programmes that serve women. Chapter I discusses the reasons that new enterprise creation is an important piece of any local economic development strategy. Chapter II describes the choices women have in the labour market and how these choices influence their decision to pursue self-employment. Chapter III takes an in-depth look at the experience of women business owners in the OECD Member countries.

Chapter I

BUSINESS CREATION AND LOCAL ECONOMIC DEVELOPMENT: WHY ENTREPRENEURSHIP SHOULD BE ENCOURAGED

Beth Siegel

For a community, entrepreneurship is a form of taking control of its own fate in the deepest sense of the word. It is the surest means of long-term survival and growth (Shapero, 1985, p.1).

INTRODUCTION

To attract resources to venture creation programmes for women, it is important to demonstrate that new business creation is a key component of local economic development and that programmes which support self-employment and venture expansion can facilitate business creation. This chapter examines the surge of interest in new enterprise development, establishes the importance of small and new businesses to local economies, provides a typology for business development activities, and offers insights into the conditions under which a business development strategy is likely to be successful.

THE SURGE OF INTEREST IN NEW ENTERPRISES AND SMALL BUSINESSES

Until the 1980s, the primary role of local government in the economic development process was to recruit outside firms to locate within their community. The tools needed to carry out this strategy were relatively straightforward. They included tax incentives to lower location costs, low-cost financing, and below market-rate land. Since a business could locate virtually anywhere, localities pursuing this approach viewed every other city and town as a potential competitor.

In this environment, the small business sector was viewed at best as a benign force — basically unimportant to economic development — and, at worst, as quite negative — inefficient and less productive than larger firms and, consequently, a hindrance to economic growth. This latter view was widely held. Moreover, while entrepreneurs at least had a "folk hero" image in the United States, in many other countries there was a marked negative attitude towards those interested in starting their own businesses.

Support for small business grew dramatically in the 1980s. Today, promoting small business and enterprise development is seen as a key component of economic development policy, and efforts to recruit large firms have become much less popular. In the United States, a White House Conference on small business issues is held annually and many economists point to small business as a key to the future of manufacturing in the U.S. In fact, almost every U.S. state has developed specialised programmes to support small businesses and new enterprise development.

In much of the rest of the world, attitudes are as positive. 1983 was declared the "Year of Small and Medium-Sized Businesses" in Europe; the European Economic Community has established a "Task Force on Small and Medium-Sized Business"; many European countries have individually developed programmes aimed at helping small businesses and new enterprise development; and "local employment initiatives" are being formed in regions throughout the continent. Media accounts have called attention to "Europe's New Entrepreneurs" (*Fortune*, 27 April 1987), "The Entrepreneurial Itch in Europe" (*D&B Reports*, Jan/Feb 1987), and the new "Small is Beautiful" attitude in the United Kingdom (*Director*, October 1987). Albert Shapero, one of the foremost international authorities on new enterprise development, wrote "The signs of the new interest (in entrepreneurship) are all around us. Government agencies and programmes for entrepreneurship and small business are proliferating all over the world" (Shapero, 1985, p. 1).

This new "entrepreneurial" orientation is due to a number of factors. First, the changes in the international economy and the decline of traditional manufacturing industries, long dominated by a few large firms, have led to serious structural changes in many regions of the industrialised nations. The large-scale job losses resulting from these changes could not be ameliorated through traditional economic development policies that were oriented towards attracting large plants. Moreover, a consequence of large plant closings has been increasing concern about "capital flight" by multinational firms. Attracting a branch plant of a large multinational corporation is no longer seen as an adequate strategy to ensure a stable source of new jobs. The failure of this traditional approach has led to a search for alternatives.

At the same time, studies on the components of job generation demonstrated the importance of new and small business as key job creators and sources of product innovation. This research encouraged a reorientation in policy. Small and new companies are now seen as critical to economic growth, and consequently their development has become an economic development policy priority.

Finally, many observers note that the growing interest in small businesses and self-employment is related to changes in values and attitudes about work. Working for a small business or the ideal of starting your own business appeals to people's interest in greater control and self-fulfilment in the workplace.

IMPORTANCE OF THE SMALL BUSINESS SECTOR TO THE ECONOMY

The primary justification for the keen pursuit of small business growth and enterprise creation has been evidence that small business is an important source of employment and job generation and that small firms are effective in developing new products that stimulate additional economic development. Economic development professionals have also found that efforts to promote small business development and self-employment can increase the resiliency of local economies and provide a new area of opportunity for individuals left out of the economic mainstream.

Small Business as Job Creators

While it is admittedly difficult to collect consistent data across countries, many studies have confirmed the importance of small businesses to the economy. Studies by the OECD in 1985 and 1986 focused on the importance of small business and self-employment. A 1985 OECD study found that firms with fewer than 20 employees contributed a substantial share of total employment in Member countries (OECD, 1985a, pp. 64-81). As shown in Table 1.1, the contribution of small firms to employment varied considerably from country to country. Even more significant, the study concludes that there has been a trend towards small firms accounting for a greater share of employment in some countries (Table 1.2); this change has been most striking in manufacturing. A 1986 OECD study found that, on average, about one OECD worker in ten in the non-agricultural sector is self-employed and that self-employment levels, while relatively stable in most European countries, were growing in Australia, Canada, Ireland, Portugal and the U.S. (OECD, 1986).

Table 1.1.   **Distribution of total employment by enterprise size**

	Firms with under 20 employees (%)	Firms with 20-99 employees (%)	Firms with over 100 employees (%)
Austria (1981)	26.2	20.9	52.8
Belgium (1983)	25.0	20.9	54.1
France (1981)	19.7	22.3	57.9
Japan (1983)	38.8	17.5	43.6
Netherlands (1982)	25.9	22.7	51.4
Sweden (1983)	15.6	12.4	71.9
United States (1977)	21.6	18.5	59.9

Source: OECD, 1985a.
Note: Data for Sweden include public sector; for France and the U.S. service sector coverage is partial; for Japan, the smallest category is 1-29 employees and second category is 30-99.

Table 1.2.   **Changes in employment shares of very small firms**

Less than 20 workers

	%
Austria (1973-1983)	3.1
Belgium (1978-1983)	1.7
France (1975-1981)	2.4
Japan (1973-1983)	1.2
Netherlands (1978-1982)	0.01
Sweden (1983-1983)	(1.8)

Source: OECD, 1985a.
Note: Data for Sweden include public sector.

In another effort to compare small business statistics across a range of countries, authors of a 1982 study reported that firms with under 500 employees accounted for 60 per cent of employment in France, 83 per cent in Italy and Ireland, and 37 per cent of employment in the U.K. In addition, this study found that "all countries which report birth and death statistics for new firms reported an increase in births in recent years" (Burns and Dewhurst, 1982).

In the U.S., by 1988 more than 50 per cent of all private-sector employees worked for companies with fewer than 100 employees (*Wall Street Journal*, 27 April 1988, p. 29). As recently as 1980, only 48 per cent were employed by such small companies. Since 1970, the number of non-farm self-employed persons in the United States has increased by 50 per cent and, by 1985, about 13.5 per cent of all workers considered themselves self-employed on a full-time or part-time basis (SBA, 1986).

Japan has also come to recognise the importance of small business. According to an article in *Asian Business*, small and medium-sized businesses in Japan employ about 74 per cent of the total industrial workforce and create about 57 per cent of total added value to products. Japan's small firms have also been more profitable than larger firms due to their flexibility, facility to adapt more quickly to market-place changes and ability to specialise (Woronoff, 1985, pp. 70-81).

The preceding statistics demonstrate the large share of jobs that small business provides in the OECD countries and the growing importance of self-employment. Other studies have shown the key role of small business in new job development. The research of David Birch in the U.S. has had the greatest impact on the way small business has been viewed throughout the world. His work in the 1970s on the "Job Generation Process" concluded that small businesses are the primary creators of new jobs. Originally, Birch attributed 82 per cent of net employment growth to firms with under 100 employees; in 1982 he revised this figure to 70 per cent. While the research of David Birch was the first to draw attention to the importance of small business to the economy, both the methodologies and the data base used in his work have been broadly criticised (Schwartz, 1987; U.S. General Accounting Office, 1986; and Reynolds, West and Finch, 1985). Nevertheless, even though the original work that focused all of the attention on small businesses was seriously flawed, the conclusion was not. The magnitude of the impact may not be as great as Birch originally estimated, but the basic conclusion remains sound: small businesses are an important generator of new jobs in the economy. These findings have been confirmed by other U.S. and European studies.

The OECD's 1985 review of job generation studies in the U.S. and in Europe concluded that there is "considerable qualitative evidence of the importance of small firms, and small establishments to job growth" (OECD, 1985a). Specific European studies include the following. A Norwegian study found that small companies with under 20 employees had a net growth in employment, while large companies had a decline. It also found that nearly 50 per cent of all new jobs created during the period 1976-1983 were the result of entrepreneurship, where most new enterprises were small-scale, independent firms (Second International Seminar on Women — Local Initiatives — Job Creation, 1987). In *France*, a study of 12 000 firms found that small enterprises made a disproportionate contribution to job growth (OECD, 1985c).

Four separate state studies in the United States also show that small businesses are key job generators. A study in Oregon found that while businesses with fewer than 20 employees accounted for only 11 per cent of manufacturing employment, they accounted for more than 40 per cent of all new manufacturing jobs. The authors concluded: "It is clear that in Oregon's manufacturing sector, it is the very small businesses — those with fewer than 20 employees — that are the most powerful job generators" (Oregon Joint Legislative Committee, 1988). A California study reported that between 1975 and 1979, establishments with fewer than 20 employees accounted for 56 per cent of the net gains in employment and that young firms (under two years old) accounted for a greater share of employment growth than older firms (Teitz, 1981). A study of job creation and destruction in the state of Pennsylvania reported that "Employment grew strongly in small establishments (under 20 employees) and declined strongly in very large establishments (over 500 employees)" (Jacobson, 1986). Finally, a study of the job generation process in Wisconsin concluded that "very small businesses (under 20 employees) dominate the job generation process" in the United States. These results were found to be true in every year and in every sector. The Wisconsin study also found that new business starts were the key to explaining the job generation of small businesses (Wisconsin Department of Development, 1984).

Small Business as Innovators

Not only does the small business sector directly create many jobs, it also creates many of the innovations that stimulate overall economic growth. While it is difficult to generalise across all industries, recent research has found that on a per-employee basis small companies (those with under 500 employees) are more innovative; that in 14 of the 35 most innovative industries small businesses accounted for more innovations; and that, while industries with many large companies are more innovative, it is the smaller companies in those industries which are more likely to produce innovations (Case, 1989).

Small Business and the Resilience of Local Economies

Providing small business assistance and entrepreneurial development can enhance the resiliency of local economies by contributing to sustainable economic growth, greater diversification of economic activity, and increased local ownership of economic resources.

In any economy there is a constant process with firms dying and new ones being born. A resilient economy is one in which there is continual entrepreneurial activity. The constant development of new businesses creates the "seeds" for long-term economic vitality.

Rather than depending on a handful of big firms to maintain the health of the local economy, the existence of a larger number of firms in a wider variety of industries makes the local economy less vulnerable to the fortunes of one firm or industry. Many communities have learned this the hard way when they experienced large-scale job losses due to one or two big factory closures.

Small and new enterprises are more likely to be owned by residents of a community. Increased local ownership means that control of economic decision-making rests with individuals who have a strong stake in the community. This usually results in greater stability of employment, more jobs going to local residents, and more profits being reinvested in the community.

Small Business and Economic Opportunities for Disadvantaged Groups

Venture development programmes can provide opportunities to individuals with entrepreneurial ability who fall outside the conventional stereotype of an entrepreneur and may lack well-developed skills and resources. For many women and low-income and minority people, starting their own small business provides them with an economic option that has not previously been available. In fact, the motivation for most enterprise programmes targeted to women is to create new ways in which women can achieve self-sufficiency, if not economic equality. Chapters IV and V examine how enterprise programmes for women can achieve these goals.

TYPES OF BUSINESS DEVELOPMENT ACTIVITIES

Initiatives to support small business and new enterprise development fit into three categories that are differentiated by their goals and the kinds of businesses they promote. Growth company strategies are designed to promote new and small businesses which have substantial job creation potential. Self-employment programmes focus on encouraging non-traditional entrepreneurs to start their own businesses and thereby create their own employment. Efforts to promote alternative business structures target their services to community businesses, cooperatives and worker-owned businesses.

The goal of growth company strategies is to generate new employment opportunities in a community by supporting small businesses with significant growth potential. These development efforts target businesses or new enterprises that export goods and services outside the community and, in some cases, firms involved in technology-oriented or high growth sectors of the economy. In general, the orientation is toward firms in the manufacturing sector. Entrepreneurs supported through these programmes are likely to have some technical and managerial skills. They often "spin off" from another business, or from a university or research and development centre.

The goal of self-employment programmes is to promote increased self-sufficiency for people experiencing unemployment and for women and minorities, who have often been denied the option of creating their own jobs, programmes are more social in orientation, offering targeted groups a channel for social mobility. The expectation is that, while each business may create only one or a few jobs, it will enable the entrepreneur to attain economic self-sufficiency, gain work experience, and develop self-confidence.

Businesses developed or supported through self-employment programmes tend to be locally oriented, such as service and retail businesses. Those communities experiencing the most serious economic problems may lack the necessary infrastructure to implement growth company strategies, but self-employment programmes may succeed. Entrepreneurs supported through self-employment programmes often have business ideas, but lack entrepreneurial experience and resources.

Finally, efforts to develop alternative business structures usually have as one of their goals empowering workers and community residents or providing social and cultural services in the community. The orientation is towards "entrepreneurship with a social purpose" (McArthur, 1986).

Businesses started through these efforts may be in any industrial sector. What is unique about these efforts is that they frequently promote non-profit enterprises, cooperatives, or worker-owned businesses. In addition, they frequently include non-profit activities such as the provision of day care and training services as part of their agendas. These businesses are often developed by unemployed individuals, those who face plant closures, and younger people frustrated with unemployment and lack of job prospects.

BUSINESS DEVELOPMENT AS A LOCAL ECONOMIC DEVELOPMENT STRATEGY

The Success of Public Efforts in Promoting Venture Creation

In the past, even those who acknowledged the importance of small business and new enterprises were sceptical about efforts to support and promote their development. Many believed that both the quality and quantity of entrepreneurial activity was as given, and that government policy could not alter the natural rate of failure amongst small businesses. These perceptions have changed. With at least a decade of experimentation in public- and private-sector efforts supporting small business development and self-employment, evidence is mounting that entrepreneurship levels can be increased and small business sector vitality can be improved through focused efforts.

For example, Catherine Ashton, Director of Community Involvement for the U.K.'s "Business in the Community" — an umbrella organisation of over 150 enterprise agencies and 100 plus corporate sponsors — has noted that, although statistics on mortality rates are difficult to obtain, "the average of one in five companies failing within 12 months of operation drops to one in twenty where an enterprise agency (an assistance intermediary) is used" (OECD, 1985b). A study of the Small Business Development Center programme of the U.S. Small Business Administration found that the programme produced a greater than expected number of business starts and a higher than expected rate of survival (Chrisman, Hoy and Robinson, 1987). Finally, a study of the Youth Enterprise Program by FAS — the industrial training authority in Ireland that provides entrepreneurial training to youth between the ages of 19 to 24 years — reported that of the 830 young people who participated in the programme since 1984, 67 per cent are now self-employed (Connor, 1985).

The experience of the Women's Economic Development Corporation (WEDCO) in St. Paul, Minnesota, demonstrates the role which women's intermediary organisations can play in promoting entrepreneurship. WEDCO provides a range of services — from intensive management assistance to financing — for women starting or growing businesses. Since 1984, WEDCO has served 3 700 women, of whom 774 have started businesses and an additional 378 have expanded businesses. Eighty-seven per cent of these enterprises are still in business, and they each provide, on average, three full-time and five part-time jobs. Since 1985, WEDCO has made one or more loans to 135 businesses through its seed capital fund. Its annual losses on loans outstanding have been only one per cent.

Programmes which successfully support new and small business development promote an entrepreneurial environment by building the technical skills of the workforce, improving the quality of the education system, increasing the availability of financing for new enterprise development, and fostering the business management skills of residents.

Some of these programmes involve a comprehensive approach to business development which integrates many of the elements described above. Other programmes focus on one tool — for example, management assistance or financing. Neither is inherently a better strategy. The most successful programmes carefully analyse local economic conditions and the local resource base, and design a programme to fit the specific constraints and opportunities in that community. A variety of successful programmes which encourage self-employment and business expansion by women are described in detail in chapters IV and V.

The Context for Public Efforts to Promote Venture Creation

Venture creation programmes can be effective and benefit local economies as long as policymakers recognise their limitations. First, economic development is a long-term process. This is clearly evident in efforts to promote the development of new businesses or to encourage self-employment. The full benefits of these programmes will not be realised overnight. If a community is facing an immediate crisis due to the large-scale loss of jobs, shorter term development approaches should be pursued in conjunction with an enterprise development strategy. Moreover, an enterprise development strategy must be given sufficient time to succeed before its effectiveness is evaluated.

In addition, it is increasingly recognised that only a small percentage of small and new businesses are responsible for generating most employment growth and developing most innovations. Many of the enterprise development strategies being pursued, particularly those which focus on self-employment, do not emphasize the types of small businesses that are most likely to create large numbers of jobs or innovations. This does not mean that these efforts are not cost-effective. It does mean that the goals for each programme must be well defined and that each programme must be evaluated relative to its own goals.

Moreover, the quality of jobs created through small business development efforts is often lower than those being lost in more traditional industries. There is evidence that jobs in the small business sector tend to pay less, have fewer benefits, and have less job security (OECD, 1985c). In establishing new programmes, attention must be paid to job quality.

It is also true that a small business development strategy has to address the high level of risk associated with business development. The supposed failure rate of small businesses is probably one of the most often quoted and least supported statistics. A recent study of failure rates noted that "Four out of five new firms fail within the first five years. This statement has been made so many times that most people believe it is true." The researchers who are quoted, in fact, found that "To put an old adage to rest, two out of five new firms survive at least six years and over half of the survivors grow" (Phillips and Kirchhoff, 1988). While the failure rate is less than commonly believed, it still represents a significant risk factor in business development efforts.

It is becoming apparent that too high a level of entrepreneurial activity may have a negative effect on the competitive position of an industry. Some analysts are beginning to respond to a potential downside of growth company strategies — the constant loss of key employees who start their own businesses. This constant transition affects the ability of larger companies to make longterm investments. Even self-employment strategies can create excessive competition if they support too many individuals offering the same product or service in one community.

Rather than negating the benefits of pursuing a local business development strategy, these limitations point to the importance for any community of pursuing a balanced approach to development. An effective economic development strategy should encompass a range of business development activities including: encouraging self-employment, supporting existing small business, increasing the competitiveness of traditional industries, and identifying and promoting potential growth industries. These activities should also be closely co-ordinated with efforts to build the community's human resource base through investments in the education system and through improved training and retraining programmes.

CONCLUSION

The growing recognition that small and new businesses are important to economic development, along with a growing disaffection with traditional development strategies focusing on large plant recruitment, has led to a surge of interest in small business development at the local level. As part of a balanced approach to economic development, the promotion of new and small enterprises can achieve important social and economic goals in a community — generating jobs, promoting innovation, diversifying the economy, developing local ownership, and offering disadvantaged groups new opportunities. As recently as ten years ago it would have been difficult to point to many examples of successful local business development programmes. During the past decade, however, such programmes have proliferated. Local initiatives to develop new and small enterprises can now be found in communities throughout the world. These initiatives cover the full range of activities to support business development: from government-sponsored management assistance programmes to grassroots self-employment programmes.

Some of the existing economic development efforts to promote new enterprise and small business development recognise that women and other groups face particular barriers in the enterprise creation process. Removing barriers that have constrained women from becoming entrepreneurs, and providing the support needed for women entrepreneurs to become successful small business owners, greatly increases the pool of entrepreneurs in any community and thereby improves the potential of any new enterprise development strategy.

REFERENCES

Burns, Paul and Jim Dewhurst (1982) *Small Business in Europe*, Macmillan Education Ltd.

Case, John (1989) "Sources of Innovation", *Inc. Magazine*, June, p.29.

Chrisman, James J., Frank Hoy and Richard Robinson, Jr. (1987) "New Venture Development: The Costs and Benefits of Public Sector Assistance", *Journal of Business Venturing*, 2 (4), pp. 315-328.

Connor, Patrick J. (1985) "The Facilitation and Stimulation of Entrepreneurship of Young Persons in Ireland Through the Youth Enterprise Programme", *Frontiers of Entrepreneurial Research*, ed. John A. Hornaday, Edward B. Shils, Jeffry A. Timmons and Karl H. Vesper, Center for Entrepreneurial Studies, Babson College, Wellesley, Mass.

Jacobson, Louis (1986) "Job Creation and Destruction in Pennsylvania 1975-1985", The Upjohn Institute, 17 November.

McArthur, Andrew A. (1986) "An Unconventional Approach to Economic Development: The Role of Community Business", *Town Planning Review*, I (January).

OECD (1985a) "Employment in Small and Large Firms: Where Have the Jobs Come From?', *OECD Employment Outlook*.

OECD (1985b) "High-level International Conference on the Role of Large Firms in Job Creation and Entrepreneurship", Paris, 18 November.

OECD (1985c) *Creating Jobs at the Local Level*, Paris.

OECD (1986) "Self-Employment in OECD Countries", *OECD Employment Outlook*.

Oregon Joint Legislative Committee on Trade and Economic Development (1988) "Small is Bountiful: Manufacturing, Small Business and Oregon's Economy", Staff Report, 19 January.

Phillips, Bruce D. and Bruce A. Kirchhoff (1988) "Analysis of New Firm Survival and Growth", Babson Entrepreneurship Research Conference, Calgary, Canada, May 1988.

Reynolds, Paul D., Steven West and Michael D. Finch (1985) "Estimating New Firms and New Jobs: Considerations in Using the Dun and Bradstreet Files", *Frontiers of Entrepreneurial Research*, ed. John A. Hornaday, Edward B. Shils, Jeffry A. Timmons and Karl H. Vesper, Center for Entrepreneurial Studies, Babson College, Wellesley, Mass.

SBA (U.S. Small Business Administration) (1986) *State of Small Business*, U.S. Government Printing Office, 1986.

Shapero, Albert (1985) "Why Entrepreneurship: A Worldwide Perspective", *Journal of Small Business Management* (October), pp. 1-5.

Teitz, Michael (1981) "Small Business and Employment Growth in California", University of California, Berkeley, California, March.

U.S. General Accounting Office (1986) "Dislocated Workers: Extent of Business Closures, Layoffs, and the Public and Private Response", July.

Wisconsin Department of Development (Division of Policy Development, Bureau of Research) (1984) "The Job Generation Process in Wisconsin 1969-1981", December.

Woronoff, Jon (1985) *Asian Business*, 21 (4), April, pp. 70-81.

Chapter II

WOMEN IN THE LABOUR MARKET: THE CHOICES WOMEN HAVE
Julianne Malveaux

INTRODUCTION

To understand why women are choosing self-employment and how local enterprise programmes should be designed to benefit women, it is necessary to examine first the current status of women in the labour market.

Women are the primary wage-earners in many families throughout the OECD countries. One-fifth of all women are household heads in Western Europe and the U.S. (Paukert, 1982), with the rate being more than double that for Black women in the U.S. (Wallace, 1980). In many U.S. families, women's wages determine whether or not families live in poverty. Women have also had to assume more responsibility for generating family incomes as male wages have stagnated.

Since World War II, women in OECD countries have increased their labour force participation by at least one-third. Many women have joined the labour force because of economic necessity. Others have sought to exercise their right to an equal role with men in the world economy. As women's presence in the global labour market has increased, governmental and intergovernmental units have established advisory bodies on the status of women and passed laws which address the access of women to employment opportunities. These laws have made a positive contribution to the status of women, but they have not made equal employment a reality. Gaps between male and female pay, employment and occupational status, though shrinking, exist in every OECD country. These labour market realities, both positive and negative, play a role in explaining the interest which women exhibit in self-employment and their entrepreneurial potential.

Chapter II describes the status of women in the labour market (including employment, unemployment, occupations and earnings), the impact of women's growing labour force participation on the social and economic structure of the OECD countries, and the implications for women and self-employment.

EMPLOYMENT AND UNEMPLOYMENT OF WOMEN

Labour Force Participation

The increase in women's labour market participation has been dramatic. Table 2.1 shows both total labour force growth and female labour force growth in fifteen countries. Except for

Table 2.1. Women's labour force and women's employment as a share of total employment

Thousands[a], 1968-1988

	1968	1988	86/68[b]		1968	1988	88/68[b]
Canada				*Italy*			
Labour force	8 051	13 353	2.6		21 039	24 379	0.7
Women's labour force	2 598	5 861	4.2		6 003	8 832	1.9
Women's share of total employment	32.7	43.8			28.2	34.3	
United States				*Netherlands[c]*			
Labour force	82 272	123 893	2.1		5 003[d]	6 641	..
Women's labour force	29 242	54 963	3.2		1 339[d]	2 541	..
Women's share of total employment	36.6	45.0			27.5[d]	37.4	
Japan				*Norway[e]*			
Labour force	50 610	61 660	1.0		1 528	2 183	..
Women's labour force	20 030	24 730	1.1		449	974	..
Women's share of total employment	39.6	40.1			30.2	45.3	
Australia				*Portugal[f]*			
Labour force	5 219	7 962	2.1		3 525	4 616	..
Women's labour force	1 626	3 211	3.5		775	1 952	..
Women's share of total employment	31.2	40.4			n.a.	42.0	
Finland				*Spain[c, h]*			
Labour force	2 189	2 583	0.8		13 049[g]	14 972	..
Women's labour force	936	1 216	1.3		3 129[g]	5 057	..
Women's share of total employment	44.6	48.2			25.0[g]	31.2	
France				*Sweden[i]*			
Labour force	20 870	24 153	0.7		3 822	4 471	0.8
Women's labour force	7 317	10 268	1.7		1 457	2 147	2.0
Women's share of total employment	35.4	42.0			38.2	48.0	
Germany[c]				*United Kingdom*			
Labour force	26 291	29 596	..		25 378	28 211	0.5
Women's labour force	9 500	11 631	..		8 814	11 848	1.5
Women's share of total employment	36.9	39.5			35.7	40.5	

Ireland

Labour force	1 123	1 310	0.8
Women's labour force	289	400	1.6
Women's share of total employment	26.5	32.5	

a) Women's share of total employment = $\dfrac{\text{Women's civilian employment (\%)}}{\text{Total civilian employment}}$

b) Column three (88/68) shows the compounded annual growth rate of the overall labour force and the women's labour force respectively, between 1968 and 1988. Where significant breaks in the series exist, the growth rates have not been calculated.

c) Break in series between 1986 and 1987.

d) Figures refer to 1975.

e) Break in series between 1971 and 1972.

f) Break in series between 1973 and 1974.

g) Figures refer to 1970.

h) Break in series between 1975 and 1976. Data previous to 1976 refer to persons in the labour force aged 14 years and over, from 1976 they refer to persons aged 16 years and over. Data include Ceuta and Melilla.

i) Figures previous to 1986 represent all persons aged 16 to 74 years old; from 1986, figures represent all persons aged 16 to 64 years old.

.. Not calculated.

n.a. Not available.

Source: OECD, *Labour Force Statistics*, 1990.

23

Japan, the female labour force grew far more rapidly than the total labour force. It grew five times as quickly in Spain, three times as quickly in the U.K., and more than twice as quickly in Sweden, France and Germany. In general, male labour force participation rates were constant or falling between 1966 and 1989, while female labour force participation rose during the same time period.

Rough cross-national comparisons of female labour force participation are possible using the data in Table 2.2. Women's labour force participation grew most rapidly in Canada, Sweden and Norway, with female labour force participation rates higher in Sweden — at more than 83 per cent — than in any other OECD country. While the increase in women's labour force participation was slight in Japan, Ireland and Germany, it exceeded 1 per cent per year in nine of the fifteen OECD countries for which the data was available.

Table 2.2. **Women's participation rates in selected OECD countries (%)**

	1968	1989	Percentage point change
Canada	39.9	68.2	28.3
United States	48.4	69.4	21.0
Japan	56.1	59.3	3.2
Australia	43.5	60.6	17.1
Finland	60.0	73.5	13.5
France[a]	49.3	57.6	8.3
Germany[b]	47.7	54.5[c]	6.8
Ireland	34.1[d]	37.5[e]	3.4
Italy[f]	29.4	44.0	14.6
Netherlands[b]	30.4[d]	51.1	20.7
Norway	51.6[g]	72.9	21.3
Portugal	52.1[h]	58.7	6.6
Spain	31.6[g]	41.3	9.7
Sweden[b]	57.8	83.2	25.4
United Kingdom	53.5[i]	66.0	12.5

a) Break in series between 1981 and 1982.
b) Break in series between 1986 and 1987
c) Data refers to 1987.
d) Data refers to 1971.
e) Data refers to 1988.
f) Break in series between 1976 and 1977.
g) Data refers to 1972.
h) Data refers to 1974.
i) Data refers to 1970.
j) Break in series between 1970 and 1971.
Due to breaks in the series, the data are not strictly comparable, and therefore the percentage point change must be used with caution
Sources: OECD, Labour Force Statistics, Part III, 1988 and 1990.

The increase in labour market participation has not been equally dramatic for all women. It has been substantial for married women and mothers (who were less likely to have worked outside the home in the past), but much less dramatic for minority and immigrant populations (who were more likely to have worked outside the home in the past). In the U.S., for example, the labour force participation rate of Black women has always exceeded that of White women. Since Black men were unable to earn the family wages that White men earned, the wages of Black women were a critical component of Black family income. The gap between Black and White women's participation rates was more than 15 percentage points in 1960. By 1988, the gap had narrowed to about two percentage points.

The potential for women's labour force participation is even greater than the preceding statistics suggest because definitions of labour market terms sometimes misrepresent the facts. The labour force is made up of those who are "working or looking for work". The term "looking for work" is subject to misinterpretation due to the "discouraged worker" effect. Discouraged workers are those potential workers who stop seeking work when they think their chances of finding it are nil. Because discouraged workers are not included, there is an undercount in the size of the labour force and the unemployment rate. For example, in Australia, there were 113 200 discouraged job seekers in 1983 of whom 84.8 per cent were women (OECD, 1985).

Women may be especially affected by this definitional problem because many do not seek work when they cannot find affordable child care. Studies show that lack of child care is the most frequent reason why U.S. women who receive public assistance say they are not in the labour force (Lopes and View, 1983). Even estimates of discouraged workers may tend to undercount women. In Australia, 397 400 women did not seek employment at all for reasons which included lack of child care (OECD, 1985, p. 21).

Employment and Unemployment

The increases in labour force participation attained by women have translated into increases in women's employment share, as shown in Table 2.1. More than 40 per cent of all jobs are held by women in a number of OECD countries (OECD, 1989). With the exceptions of Ireland and Spain, women hold at least a third of the paid jobs in the countries shown. In Sweden and Finland, women hold nearly half of all paid jobs.

Unfortunately, women have entered labour markets that accommodate more unemployment than they did twenty years ago. This upward trend in unemployment has affected every country shown in Table 2.3. While the unemployment rates are lower in 1989 in some of the countries than they were in 1985, they are still much higher than they were two decades earlier.

In general, women's unemployment rates are higher than those of men. This is true for most of the countries included in Table 2.3, as well as for other OECD countries. It is important to note that these data are not strictly comparable across countries because definitions of unemployment differ (Paukert, 1982, p. 8). The degree to which women's unemployment exceeds that of men may be understated in the statistics of many countries. Discouraged workers who drop out of the labour force explain undercounts in the women's unemployment rate in the U.S. In the U.K., on the other hand, "not all unemployed women are included in the registered unemployed figures because they do not register as unemployed even if they are seeking work" (Paukert, 1982). As in other labour force research, employment and unemployment statistics are defined and developed with little consideration of the fact that women must balance their work efforts with family responsibilities.

Aggregate women's unemployment rates also fail to capture differences in unemployment among diverse groups of women. Black women in the U.S. have unemployment rates that are nearly twice those of White women, while Hispanic women have rates that are about 50 per cent higher than White women's rates. The economic status of these women is eroded by not only the high unemployment rates they experience, but also by the likelihood that they will work part-time.

Table 2.3. **Unemployment rates in selected OECD countries**

Percentages

	1968	1975	1985	1989
Canada				
Total	5.9[e]	6.9	10.4	7.5
Men	6.6[e]	6.2	10.3	7.3
15-24	12.6[e]	12.5	18.1	12.4
25-54	4.8[e]	4.3	8.4	6.1
Women	4.5[e]	8.1	10.6	7.8
15-24	7.7[e]	11.4	14.4	10.0
25-54	2.9[e]	6.7	9.7	7.5
United States				
Total	3.4	8.3	7.1	5.2
Men	2.7	7.6	6.8	5.1
16-24	6.2	15.1	13.1	10.6
25-54	1.6	5.5	5.4	4.0
Women	4.8	9.3	7.4	5.3
16-24	9.7	15.4	12.9	10.3
25-54	3.4	7.4	6.2	4.4
Japan				
Total	1.2	1.9	2.6	2.2
Men	1.2	2.0	2.6	2.2
15-24	1.9	3.5	4.8	4.7
25-54	1.0	1.6	1.9	1.5
Women	1.1	1.8	2.7	2.3
15-24	1.9	2.6	4.7	4.2
25-54	1.0	1.7	2.4	2.2
Australia				
Total	1.6	4.6	7.9	5.7
Men	1.0	3.5	7.8	5.4
15-24	2.0	7.5	15.1	10.0
25-54	0.7	2.3	5.6	4.0

	1968	1975	1985	1989
France				
Total	1.9	3.7	10.1	9.5
Men	1.5	2.7	8.3	7.1
15-24	2.7	6.1	21.6	14.8
25-54	1.1	2.0	6.1	6.0
Women	2.5	5.4	12.6	12.6
15-24	4.0	10.1	30.5	24.2
25-54	2.2	4.3	9.4	11.3
Germany[a]				
Total	0.7	3.7	7.7	7.1[b]
Men	0.7	3.2	6.6	6.1[b]
15-24	0.3	4.9	8.1	7.2[b]
25-54	0.4	2.9	5.8	5.5[b]
Women	0.6	4.6	9.5	8.8[b]
15-24	0.6	5.7	11.3	9.0[b]
25-54	0.6	4.3	8.7	8.5[b]
Ireland[c]				
Total	6.9[f]	9.3	17.3	16.7
Men	7.5[f]	9.8	18.8	18.6
15-24	10.7[f]	15.7	26.4	27.9
25-54	5.9[f]	8.4	17.8	17.3
Women	5.0[f]	8.0	13.8	12.3
15-24	7.0[f]	12.2	21.2	20.9
25-54	3.4[f]	5.4	8.9	7.8
Italy				
Total	3.5	3.3	10.3	12.0
Men	3.3	2.8	6.8	8.1
14-24	10.7	12.5	28.0	27.8
25-59	2.0	1.4	3.2	4.9

Women				
15-24	2.8	6.5	8.0	6.2
25-54	3.3	10.8	13.3	10.8
	2.8	4.7	6.0	4.7
Finland				
Total	3.9	2.6	5.0	3.5
Men				
15-24	5.7	2.7	5.5	3.6
25-54	9.4	5.1	9.4	6.0
	4.7	2.2	4.6	3.1
Women				
15-24	1.6	2.5	4.6	3.4
25-54	2.3	5.1	8.7	6.2
	1.5	1.7	3.2	2.6
Norway				
Total	1.6[h]	2.2	2.7	4.9
Men				
16-24	1.3[h]	1.7	2.2	5.1
25-59	5.3[h]	7.9	5.8	11.9
	0.5[h]	0.8	1.5	3.9
Women				
16-24	2.1[h]	2.9	3.2	4.7
25-59	4.9[h]	7.6	7.4	10.9
	1.4[h]	1.7	2.5	3.5
Portugal				
Total	1.7[g]	4.9	8.1	4.9
Men				
15-24	1.2[g]	4.4	6.1	3.3
25-54	3.3[g]	8.8	15.3	8.4
	0.6[g]	3.4	4.2	2.3
Women				
15-24	2.4[g]	5.8	11.0	7.1
25-54	5.1[g]	11.1	24.6	15.0
	1.4[g]	3.8	7.8	5.8
Spain				
Total	2.0[h]	4.3	21.2	17.0
Men				
15-24	2.1[h]	4.6	19.6	12.7
25-54	4.6[h]	9.8	39.3	24.4
	1.6[h]	3.4	15.4	10.0
Women				
16-24	1.5[h]	3.7	25.0	25.4
25-54	2.8[h]	7.8	51.0	42.6
	0.9[h]	1.8	16.0	21.2

Women				
14-24	4.1	4.6	16.7	18.7
25-59	10.3	13.2	40.9	40.4
	1.9	2.0	9.6	13.0
Netherlands[a]				
Total	1.3[f]	3.9	13.1	9.8
Men				
15-24	1.4[f]	4.2	13.1	8.7
25-54	2.0[f]	8.0	23.3	9.3
	1.2[f]	3.5	11.6	6.3
Women				
15-24	0.9[f]	3.1	13.1	11.6
25-54	0.8[f]	4.3	22.6	13.7
	1.0[f]	2.2	9.4	11.1
Sweden[a]				
Total	2.2	1.6	2.8	1.3
Men				
16-24	2.3	1.3	2.8	1.3
25-54	3.7	2.8	5.8	3.0
	1.7	0.8	2.0	1.0
Women				
16-24	2.2	2.0	2.9	1.4
25-54	4.3	4.8	5.7	3.0
	1.6	1.4	1.9	1.0
United Kingdom[d]				
Total	2.2[e]	3.9	12.4	6.3
Men				
16-24	2.9[e]	5.1	14.4	8.0
25-54	3.6[e]	10.3	24.3	10.5
	2.2[e]	3.6	11.6	7.2
Women				
16-24	0.8[e]	2.1	9.5	4.2
25-54	1.7[e]	6.5	18.7	6.5
	0.5[e]	0.9	6.5	3.5

a) Break in series between 1986 and 1987.
b) Figures are for 1987.
c) Figures are for 1988.
d) Break in series between 1981 and 1982.
e) Figures are for 1970.
f) Figures are for 1971.
g) Figures are for 1974.
h) Figures are for 1972.
Sources: OECD, *Labour Force Statistics*, Part III, 1988 and 1990.

Unemployment rates for women relative to those for men are unlikely to fall in the near future. In fact, many women will be faced with job loss as a result of technological change, especially in offices where women workers are concentrated, as indicated by studies from France, Germany, the U.K. and the U.S. (Wernke, 1983, p. 17). Women may find their job options diminished partly as the range of alternatives is reduced, especially where office automation leads to lay-offs, low-paying labour-intensive jobs in textiles and light manufacturing continue to be exported from industrialised to developing countries (Janjik, 1985). The OECD countries will be able to lower unemployment rates for women only if they expand their economies or if they implement training programmes to complement laws which guarantee "equal opportunity" for women in many OECD countries.

Part-time Employment

Women are more likely than men to work part-time, in some cases holding more than one part-time job. The part-time sector has expanded along with women's labour force participation, with a pronounced increase in part-time employment in the OECD countries taking place since 1973 (OECD, 1985, p. 15). In some European countries part-time jobs account for all growth in employment of women between 1979 and 1986. In 1986, women held more than 80 per cent of all part-time jobs in Belgium, Denmark, France, Germany, Norway, Sweden and the United Kingdom. Nearly half of all women workers in the Netherlands, Sweden and the U.K. worked part-time (OECD, 1988, p. 149).

Part-time employment is popular with employers because it gives them the flexibility to adjust for cyclical product or service demand and avoids the costs associated with permanent employment. One of the reasons for women's increased presence in part-time employment is their concentration in service employment, where nearly half of all jobs are part-time. A very different reason is the need that women have for flexible employment because they must juggle paid employment with family responsibilities.

The fact that women are responsible for family care raises questions about the way part-time employment is measured and defined. In the U.S., part-time workers are classified as either "voluntary" or "economic" part-time workers. By definition, economic part-time workers take part-time jobs because they can not find full-time ones. In fact, women probably have little choice when they opt for part-time work because of family responsibilities. The distinction between voluntary and economic part-time work is neither clear nor reasonable when the official definition of "economic reasons" excludes reasons most women would define as economic — the paucity of child care and the unavailability of flexible schedules. In 1987 in the U.S., more than 2 million people held part-time jobs "for economic reasons", because they would have taken full-time work were it offered (U.S. Department of Labor, 1988, p. 17). Another 11 million were described as "voluntary" part-time workers. How many, given the appropriate child care arrangements, would have opted for full-time employment?

The high incidence of part-time work among women is especially troubling because so many of these women are household heads and the sole support of their families. Part-time workers, depending on the number of hours that they work, do not generally qualify for health insurance and other benefits. In Great Britain, part-time workers do not benefit from reforms, such as maternity leave, because of their part-time status (Lorwin and Boston, 1985, p. 149). Benefits are scarce even though many part-time workers hold more than one job, or, as is the case in Japan, work as many hours as full-time workers (Hayashi, 1985, p. 58).

Despite the economic disadvantages, there have been efforts in some OECD countries to promote part-time work because it makes it easier for mothers to manage paid employment and household work. Hanna Beate Schopp-Schilling wrote that part-time employment is promoted in Germany because it is the only means to "combine family work and employment" (1985, p. 135). On the other hand, Andrée Michel describes part-time work as "not a desired benefit but an obstacle to the realisation of equality between the sexes at work" in France (1985, p. 116).

It is important to distinguish between low-paying part-time work that offers few benefits and job-sharing arrangements that allow women to earn proportional benefits for part-time work. In the U.S., the organisation "New Ways To Work" has been an advocate for reduced work time employment options, providing advice to employers and workers about ways to negotiate such schedules (New Ways to Work, 1988).

OCCUPATIONS AND EARNINGS

The occupational segregation of women into a few, low-paying jobs has been an aspect of women's employment that has changed, but very slowly, as women's labour force participation has increased. Though definitions and measurements of occupational segregation vary (OECD, 1985), it is clear that when women make up 42 per cent of the U.S. labour market, but more than 98 per cent of the secretaries (Bergman 1986, p. 317); or a third of all workers in Luxembourg, but 80 per cent of all service workers (Wernke, 1983, p. 29); and when 63 per cent of women workers in Austria work in just six (of 75) occupational categories (OECD, 1985), there remains an imbalance in the occupations where women and men are concentrated.

Occupational segregation is the result of a combination of protective legislation which has crowded women into less attractive employment and direct discrimination. Protective and other laws have gradually been repealed throughout the OECD countries. For example, 83 per cent of a set of Japanese businesses surveyed in 1981 had positions that were not open to women (Hayashi, 1985, p. 59). In 1984, 66 per cent (a somewhat smaller share) of all enterprises offering jobs to four-year college graduates made public job offers only to men (Matsubara, 1987, p. 9). Today, the Japanese public opposes this kind of inequality, and an Equal Employment Opportunity Law was enacted in 1986 (Matsubara, 1987, p. 13).

Even where the law does not exclude women from certain occupational options, women are often steered to "typically female" jobs by school counsellors, employers and others. Even where women work in the same occupations as men, they often work in segregated work units, at lower levels of responsibility, and assigned to a different set of tasks. Women are still much less likely than men to be employed in manufacturing or transport, and most of the progress women have made into typically male occupations has been at the entry level.

For women of colour, race is sometimes a factor in the way occupations are divided. In the U.S., Malveaux has defined the concept of "Black women's crowding" as segregation, beyond gender segregation, that can be measured for Black women. While Black and White women share segregation in clerical occupations, for example, Black women are more likely to be typists and filing clerks than legal or medical secretaries; they are also more likely to be nurse's assistants than dental aides (Malveaux, 1985).

Occupational segregation has had a comprehensive effect on the labour market status of women, affecting occupational choice, the sector of employment women (professionals, for example, are more likely to work in the federal government than in the private sector), the possibility of promotions, and, most importantly, the level of pay. Because occupational segregation crowds women into a few occupations, employers are able to suppress wages in those occupations. Although the laws of supply and demand adjust wages in response to shortages and surpluses in the general labour market, such wage adjustment tends to be much slower in occupations that are typically female. In the nursing profession, for example, employers have met the threat of labour shortages with flexible schedules and increased prerequisites, but not always with higher pay (Aiken, 1984).

While occupational segregation is significant, it has been declining slowly since 1970 in most OECD countries, with Germany and Belgium notable exceptions. In Sweden "the most extreme cases of segregation have been slightly attenuated" (Ericsson, 1985, pp. 140-141). In the U.S., the number of three-digit (detailed) occupation categories that had an insignificant (less than 0.5 per cent) number of women dropped from 92 to 56 (of 440) between 1972 and 1985. A look at the post-secondary enrolments of women, as well as their representation in law, medical and professional schools, suggests that, at least at the top, more women will work in typically male jobs in the future (OECD, 1985).

The majority of women still work in "typically female" jobs. Their job segregation limits the effectiveness of equal pay laws which apply only when men and women are doing the same work. Women are still concentrated in the lowest-paying sectors of the labour market. As a result, women's earnings, though they vary by country, range between 50 and 90 per cent of men's earnings (see Table 2.4). Some economists assert that the earnings gap is due to differences in the number of hours worked by men and women. But even when hours worked, occupation, industry, tenure and age are considered, there is a component of the pay gap which remains unexplained.

Table 2.4. **Wage differentials for manual workers in manufacturing industries, in selected OECD countries**

Ratio of women's average wage to men's average wage (%)

	1975	1986
Denmark	84.3	84.9
Finland	72.6	77.4
France	76.4	78.1
Germany	72.1	72.9
Ireland	60.9	68.7
Japan	51.6	48.5
Netherlands	79.2	78.6
Norway	78.0	85.0
Sweden	85.2	90.4
Switzerland	68.0	67.4
United Kingdom	66.5	67.9

Source: OECD, Employment Outlook, September 1988, chapter 5.

The view that, as women choose jobs that are not segregated, their pay levels will increase and the pay gap will shrink, ignores labour market realities, including the projected growth in low-wage occupations where women are heavily represented. In a few OECD countries, women are increasing their presence in higher-paid professional occupations. However, there is little reason to expect earnings advances in most jobs. In fact, the percentage of women in low-wage jobs is growing (Wagman and Folbre, 1988, p. 56).

If the pay gap is the result of institutional prejudice in the labour market, including differences in the way work is evaluated by gender, then policies are needed to facilitate institutional change. In particular, legislation that mandates equal pay (for jobs of equal value or comparable worth) could be effective in reducing the pay gap. In 1975, the European Commission issued a directive requiring Member States to pass laws mandating equal pay for work of equal value (Cook, 1985, p. 25). A few other OECD countries, like Australia and Canada, have passed comprehensive legislation, as have several local jurisdictions in the U.S. Still, despite the EEC requirement, the policy of ensuring pay equity has had a limited and uneven impact on the OECD countries, and has yet to close the pay gap shown in Table 2.4.

THE IMPACT OF WOMEN'S LABOUR FORCE PARTICIPATION

Increased labour force participation by women has changed both the social and the economic structure of the OECD countries.

Changes in the Family

"Economic, social and demographic changes in recent decades have upset the once-established dynamic of work and family life." So begins a 1986 report of the U.S. Bureau of National Affairs on work and family (BNA, 1986, p. 31). The rising labour market presence of women, says the report, has changed family life and child-raising patterns; it has also changed gender roles in the labour force.

As a result of the increase in women's labour force participation, women must now juggle paid work and family responsibilities. Women's work efforts have increased the demand for quality child care. In addition, women's presence in the labour market has created the need for parental leave policies.

Most industrialised countries now have family policies that address the need working women have for child care, child allowances and parental leave (Kammerman and Kahn, 1978). The right to paid maternity leave with the protection of employment exists in all of the European OECD countries. However, the policies of these countries vary in the amount of leave available, with 12 to 18 weeks being the norm. Finland provides 258 working days and Sweden provides nearly a year. Canada and New Zealand also provide limited benefits. However, only ten states in the U.S. mandate job protection for women who take unpaid maternity leave and there is no federally legislated protection. Nor is there a uniform maternity leave policy in Australia.

Official and unofficial ways of meeting the need for affordable child care also vary by country. In none of the countries is child care readily available to all women. Sweden has a long-term goal of providing state-supported child care for all children, but today fewer than a third of eligible children are in day care centres or municipally supported family day homes (Qvist, 1985, p. 276). In Germany, there is no government-supported child care, but a 1974 law allows parents to take five sick days per year for sick children (Cook, 1985, p. 67). The number of day care centres supported by public funds in Denmark is rising, but still can provide service to only a fraction of that nation's children (Foged, 1985, p. 56). In the U.K., some unions have bargained for workplace child care, but otherwise women must find child care on their own (Lorwin and Boston, 1985, p. 156). In Ireland, there are child care shortages and little publicly available child care (King, 1985, p. 169). In the United States, there has been little initiative on the part of federal or state governments to provide affordable child care for working women. In 1986, only 2 500 U.S. companies offered any child care assistance to employees (BNA, 1986, p. 31). Even when employers provide child care and parental leave, these benefits are frequently available only to women at the top of the occupational ladder.

Because the structure of the primary labour market is changing too slowly to accommodate the needs of working women with children, women are seeking alternative forms of work, such as flexitime, job sharing, industrial homework, non-traditional tracks to promotion and partnership, and self-employment. As long as these alternatives do not regularly generate marginal incomes or remove women from the policy-making and decision-making that takes place in primary labour markets, they may be viable alternatives to the primary labour force. Nevertheless, the development of quality and affordable child care and the implementation of laws requiring parental leave are critical if women are to reach their full potential in the labour market.

Changes in the Economy

Women's increased labour force participation has changed the economies of the OECD countries by enhancing the quality of the labour pool, reducing the risk of labour shortages, allowing more time for leisure and study, reducing the supply of undervalued volunteer labour, and creating demand for new goods and services.

Expanding the participation of women and minorities in the labour force has given OECD countries access to a larger pool of outstanding workers. In addition, when economies are expanding or labour forces are ageing, the additional labour supply due to participation by women in the labour force can assist economic expansion. This is especially true when women have equal access to education and training so that they are able to fill jobs in every field and occupation. In the U.S., for example, corporation heads have expressed concern that there will be labour shortages in the next decade (Committee for Economic Development Research and Policy, 1987, p. 4), but the non-discriminatory utilisation of both minority and female populations can ameliorate such shortages.

Unfortunately, during the period when women's labour force participation increased most, the world economy was weakened by the "oil shock" of 1973 and a world recession in the 1980s. Women have lost out to the economic crises and technological change that have affected the world economy in recent years. Countries which are grappling with stagnant growth have given little support to women's employment. Few OECD countries can fully employ their working-age citizens.

The rise in women's labour force participation has increased the time available for leisure and study in the OECD countries. In the U.S., the decline in labour force participation for White men has been attributed to men taking advantage of leisure and study opportunities, as demonstrated by a rise in early retirements and delayed labour force entries. (In contrast, Black men in the U.S. have experienced lower participation rates because of discrimination and their concentration in sectors of the economy which have declined.)

As the supply of women workers has risen, the supply of unpaid volunteers has declined. The critical social services which have been provided to society by women volunteers have always been undervalued in calculating country GNP to include the value of paid labour only. The value of women's work in the home, as unpaid family workers in family-owned businesses, as volunteers,

32

and in the informal sector of the economy has not been assessed. Yet, as women shift their participation to the paid labour force, the impact on these sectors may be significant.

Finally, women's work creates demand for many goods and services, including child care services and labour-saving appliances and services. In the long run, women's increased labour force participation will create additional employment and entrepreneurial opportunities.

In spite of the actual and potential contribution of women to OECD country economies, the economic climate of the 1990s poses serious challenges for women workers. As governments attempt to balance their budgets, and corporations focus on maintaining and increasing their profits, there may be fewer resources available to support women's employment.

Laws and social reforms have narrowed the gap between men and women, but they have not eliminated it. The slow pace of change in opportunity, especially for women in low paying, typically female occupations, suggests that gender parity will not happen solely because of economic expansion, but only if it is identified as a key public policy goal. Until this happens, many more women may turn to self-employment to achieve their economic potential. The majority of their businesses are likely to be in sectors where women have typically been employed.

Women and Self-employment

Since women account for a growing share of the labour force, it is not surprising that the women's share of total self-employment has risen on average in the OECD countries. In 1969 the unweighted average proportion of women among the self-employed was 24.1 per cent. By 1986, it was 28.4 per cent (OECD, 1988, p. 150).

Limited employment opportunities and persistent occupational segregation have provided additional incentives for women to turn to self-employment. When women cannot gain access to higher paying jobs, some create their own jobs. For example, the rapid pace with which women in the U.S. have established businesses — at twice the rate of overall business growth — is partly attributed to the realisation by well-educated, highly skilled women, that so-called "glass ceilings" limit their progress in the corporate world.

Self-employment can offer opportunities for increased income and job satisfaction. While many self-employed individuals have relatively low earnings, the percentage of women who earn more than men is higher among those who are self-employed. High incomes for women are considerably more frequent in self-employment than in dependent employment (OECD, 1988, pp. 157-162).

Self-employment also can offer greater job flexibility. Some women choose self-employment (which is also frequently part-time employment) because they need this flexibility to meet their continued family responsibilities. Self-employment more easily accommodates flexible working hours. In addition, many of the "traditional" skills women acquire lend themselves to self-employment. For example, women have created successful catering businesses out of their homes.

For all the opportunity and flexibility that self-employment offers, it is important to note that many self-employed women share low wages and unstable work arrangements with their sisters who are employed in the private sector. Like other women workers, self-employed women earn less than similarly employed men. Initiatives to promote women's self-employment must offer women the potential to earn a living wage, and to enjoy the same types of profit potential as male entrepreneurs.

33

CONCLUSION

The growing interest among OECD Member countries in enterprise creation programmes which serve women is a logical result of the changing labour market role of women. Women account for a growing share of the labour market in the OECD countries. In their search for economic equality they are pursuing all forms of employment, including self-employment. As the data show, however, the average woman in the labour force experiences more unemployment than her male counterpart, earns less, works in a traditionally female occupation, is more likely to work part-time, and has primary family responsibilities along with her paid employment. Despite improvements in women's status, there remain pay gaps, occupation gaps and unemployment gaps. Given these labour market realities, it is not surprising that women are turning to self-employment as one means to expand their opportunities.

To improve the status of women in the labour market, family and social policy reforms must be combined with the labour market policies of comparable worth, educational access, equal opportunity and anti-discriminatory legislation. These policies will also enhance the entrepreneurial potential of women. In fact, policies which eliminate occupational segregation, provide women with equal access to education, and improve access to child care, can substantially increase the effectiveness of enterprise creation programmes which serve women.

REFERENCES

Aiken, L. (1984) "Nursing Labor Market", *Journal of Nursing Administration*, 14, pp. 18-23.

Bergmann, B. (1986) *The Economic Emergence of Women*, Basic Books, New York.

BNA (U.S. Bureau of National Affairs) (1986) *Work and Family: A Changing Dynamic*, Washington, D.C.

Committee for Economic Development Research and Policy (1987) *Children in Need: Investment Strategies for the Educationally Disadvantaged*, Council on Economic Development, New York.

Cook, A. *et al.* (1985) *Women in Trade Unions in Eleven Industrialized Countries*, Temple University Press, Philadelphia.

Cook, A. (1985) "Introduction" and "Germany", in Cook *et al.*

Ericsson, Y. (1985) "Sweden", in Farley.

Farley, J. (ed.) (1985) *Women Workers in Fifteen Countries*, ILR Press, Ithaca, N.Y.

Foged, B. *et al.* (1985) "Denmark", in Cook *et al.*

Hayashi, H. (1985) "Japan", in Farley.

King, D. (1985) "Ireland", in Cook et al.

Janjik, M. (1985) "Women's Work in Industrialized Countries: An Overview from the Perspective of the International Labour Organisation", in Farley.

Kammerman, S. and A. Kahn (1978) *Family Policy: Government and Families in Fourteen Countries*, Columbia Press, New York.

Lopes, M. and J. View (1983) *Women, Welfare, and Enterprise*, American Enterprise Institute, Washington, D.C.

Lorwin, V. and S. Boston (1985) "Great Britain", in Cook *et al.*

Malveaux, J. (1985) "The Economic Interest of Black and White Women: Are They Similar?", *Review of Black Political Economy*, 14 (1).

Matsubara, N. (1987) "Equal Employment programmes and Policies: Japan", mimeo, International Labour Affairs Division, Ministry of Labour, Tokyo, Japan.

Michel, A. (1985) "France", in Farley.

New Ways to Work (1988) "Wanted: Equitable Conditions for Part-Time and Temporary Work", mimeo, New Ways To Work, San Francisco, CA.

OECD (1985) *The Integration of Women into the Economy*, Paris.

OECD (1988) *OECD Employment Outlook*, September, Paris.

OECD (1989) *Labour Force Statistics 1967-1987*, Paris.

Paukert, L. (1982) "Personal Preference, Social Change, or Economic Necessity? Why Women Work.", *Labour and Society*, 7 (4).

Qvist, G. et al. (1985) "Sweden", in Cook *et al.*

Schopp-Schilling, H.B. (1985) "Federal Republic of Germany", in Farley.

U.S. Department of Labor, Bureau of Labor Statistics (1988) "Employment and Earnings", 35 (1), Washington, D.C., p. 17.

Wagman, B. and N. Folbre (1988) "The Feminization of Inequality: Some New Patterns", *Challenge Magazine*, November-December, p. 56.

Wallace, P. (1980) *Black Women in the Labor Force*, MIT Press, Cambridge, Mass.

Wernke, D. (1983) *Microelectronics and Office Jobs: The Impact of the Chip on Women's Employment*, ILO, Geneva.

Chapter III

WOMEN AND ENTERPRISE CREATION

Candida Brush

AN OVERVIEW OF WOMEN-OWNED BUSINESSES

The woman business owner is increasingly visible in the local economies of all 24 OECD countries (OECD, 1987). The rapid rise in the number of women-owned businesses since 1970 represents one of the most significant economic and social developments in the world. New technologies, advances in communication, and greater acceptance of working women have created opportunities for women to start businesses in areas such as software production, clothing manufacturing, construction, and publishing.

Examples of women business owners include an Irish inventor of a high technology electronic quality control machine who employs 14 people to manufacture the device; an American lawyer who left her profession out of frustration and started up a landscaping and nursery business; a Japanese housewife who transferred her domestic skills to a business in which she teaches Japanese cooking to foreign workers; and a French blue-collar worker who lost her job due to factory closing and united with co-workers to purchase and operate the company.

In spite of recent progress, women as business owners have not received the attention they deserve from national and local governments, educational institutions, or the business and financial communities.

As a result of socio-cultural, economic and regulatory traditions, women face barriers to obtaining information and financing that are often exacerbated by their educational and occupational backgrounds, income level and race. Similarly, while the proportion of women in self-employment has risen internationally, the proportion of women with relatively low earnings has also been growing (OECD, 1988, E3).

This chapter describes the growth of women-owned business in the 24 OECD countries, points out similarities and differences in businesses across countries and industry sectors, examines the implications of women's occupational experiences and educational backgrounds, discusses the barriers and opportunities women face at business start-up, and briefly summarises current policies directed towards women's business development.

Presence of Women Business Owners

Identifying women business owners from available government statistics in OECD countries is fraught with problems due to differing classifications of businesses. Terms used to categorise

37

women's businesses include: unincorporated self-employed, incorporated self-employed, independent self-employed, employers, new entrepreneurship, and female-owned sole proprietorships. Further, the same term may not be used consistently; for example, self-employed may include subcontractors working for other employers as well as independently employed individuals. Similarly, the term "entrepreneur" may include small businesses (Canada), new firms (Germany), or a combination of employers and self-employed (Finland). The difficulties encountered when comparing different units of analysis are exacerbated when examining women-owned businesses because there are often few data available. In many cases, the most recent statistics on self-employed women or the number of businesses created by women are three or more years old.

For purposes of this discussion, the term "woman business owner" will be used to encompass other terms noted above. Where statistics are particular to a specific definition used by a country, the term applying to that country will be used (see note 1).

In most OECD countries, men constitute the majority of the self-employed population (see note 2 and Table 3.1). A look at non-agricultural self-employment by age and gender in 19 OECD countries shows that women represent, on average, 25 per cent of the total number of self-employed persons. The greatest percentages are found in Canada and the U.S., with the lowest in Denmark, Greece and Luxembourg. In all countries, 25-54 years is the predominant age group for the self-employed.

More importantly, available OECD country reports show that the number of businesses created by women is growing, often at a rate faster than for men. Further, the growth in the number of women-owned businesses is expected to continue in all OECD countries (OECD, 1987;

Table 3.1. **Composition of non-agricultural self-employment by sex, 1988**[a]

	Total (thousands)	Men (%)	Women (%)
Australia	863	68.6	31.4
Austria	193	n.a	n.a
Belgium	450	71.6	28.7
Canada	851	60.9	39.1
Denmark	158	n.a	n.a
France[b]	2 097	n.a	n.a
Germany[c]	1 929	76.8	23.2
Greece	737	82.8	17.2
Ireland	119	n.a	n.a
Italy	4 136	77.1	22.8
Japan	6 890	64.3	35.7
Netherlands	439	n.a	n.a
Norway	126	73.0	27.8
Spain	1 830	74.1	25.9
Sweden	285	74.4	26.3
United Kingdom	2 718	74.3	25.7
United States	8 474	65.2	34.8

a) Data refer to civilian employment.
b) Figures include unpaid family workers.
c) Figures refer to 1986.
n.a. not available.
Source: OECD, *Labour Force Statistics*, 1990.

Silvestri and Lucasiewiecz, 1987). The greatest increase has been in the U.S., where the annual increase in female self-employment in non-farm sole proprietorships grew by 56 per cent (versus 26 per cent for men) between 1975 and 1985 (OECD, 1986). The U.S. Small Business Administration (SBA) estimated in 1974 that there were 1.9 million women-owned, non-farm businesses including partnerships, corporations and sole proprietorships, while 1984 figures showed the number to be 3.3 million. This represents an increase of about 9.4 per cent per year (versus 4.3 per cent for men).

Similar trends are reported for other OECD countries (see note 3). In Canada, in 1980, women owned three times more businesses than in 1964, and they currently own one-third of all businesses. In Sweden, 18 per cent of all entrepreneurs are women and their number grew at an annual rate of about 9 per cent between 1972 and 1982. The Netherlands notes an increase of 36 per cent between 1975 and 1985 for women-owned businesses, whose owners comprise 20 per cent of the active entrepreneurial population. According to a Labour Force Survey in Great Britain, the number of women-owned businesses is growing at a rate of about 10 per cent per year and the total increased by 50 per cent between 1981 and 1986. Between 1981 and 1983 the percentage of self-employed women in Great Britain increased by 24 per cent, as compared with 2 per cent for men during the same period (Goffee and Scase, 1987, p. 4). In Germany, every third new firm is founded by a woman. Self-employment of women in the Federal Republic increased by 4 per cent between 1980 and 1985, and currently women account for nearly 30 per cent of all self-employed. Finnish women entrepreneurs account for about 20 per cent of all entrepreneurs (in all areas except agriculture) and their number increased by about 4 per cent between 1960-1980. In Australia, the growth of self-employment for men and women was the same between 1980 and 1986, and it is estimated that 6.4 per cent of all employed women are entrepreneurs. Belgium, Norway and Italy also report growth in self-employment of women in the 5 to 15 per cent range since 1981. Similarly, in Greece and Portugal, the numbers of self-employed women and women employers has increased since 1975 (Halpern, 1987, p. 23). In France, the percentage of women employers increased from 17.4 per cent in 1982 to 22 per cent in 1984. Norwegian labour market statistics show that the proportion of new entrepreneurship registered by women has increased from 14 per cent in 1982 to 19 per cent in 1985.

Sector of Industry

Across all OECD countries, the great majority of women-owned businesses are concentrated in the retail trade and service sectors, which are traditional areas of female employment. Estimates based on a survey of 17 000 women in several European countries (excluding Spain and Portugal) show nearly 5 million women are self-employed. Of these, approximately 46 per cent are in retail trade, 12 per cent in beauty and health care, 10 per cent in liberal professions, 9 per cent in agriculture, 9 per cent handicrafts, and only 1 per cent in industry (CREW, 1987).

On a country-by-country basis, the distributions are similar (see Table 3.2). A study in the Netherlands revealed that 59 per cent of women-owned businesses were in personal services, banking, finance, insurance and other services, while 32 per cent were in distribution, hotels, catering and repair. In Australia, approximately 69 per cent of the country's 150 000 self-employed women operate businesses in the retail trade, recreation, and personal services sectors. Germany, Great Britain, Norway and Finland also report that the majority of women-owned firms are in the retail trades, hotel, restaurant and personal services sectors. In the U.S., services account for 50 per cent, and retail trade 30 per cent of all female-owned sole proprietorships (SBA, 1985, p. 295).

Table 3.2. **Percentage of women in self-employment according to activity — 1984**

	Belgium	Denmark	Germany	Greece	Ireland	Italy	Netherlands	Portugal	Spain
Agriculture	7.8	-6.2	12.3	36.3	37.1	25.6	9.0	59.9	32.1
Mines	2.7	—	—	—	—	—	—	—	—
Industry	0.1	10.5	10.2	13.7	2.9	12.0	4.0	9.7	8.1
Gas-electricity	0.6	0.8	—	0.1	—	0.1	—	0.1	0.2
Building	—	—	—	0.1	2.4	0.2	0.5	—	—
Restoration	63.0	35.7	46.3	24.2	43.9	47.8	42.5	25.6	46.9
Transport	0.5	0.7	1.8	0.6	0.8	0.4	0.7	0.1	0.1
Communications	—	—	—	—	—	—	—	—	—
Finance	5.9	7.1	6.8	5.6	2.5	3.1	8.6	0.4	1.1
Services	19.5	39.0	21.5	16.0	12.8	10.5	33.6	3.9	11.5
Services to people	—	—	—	—	—	—	—	—	—
Other activities	—	—	—	0.1	0.1	—	1.5	0.1	—
Total	100.0	100.0	100.0	100.0	100.0	100.0	100.0	100.0	100.0

Note: Data for France and Luxembourg are not available.
Source: EUROSTAT

General economic and industrial factors in each OECD country impact the types of business created by women. For instance, because New Zealand, Finland, Austria and Norway have large farming, fishing and agriculture industries, a relatively higher proportion of women own businesses in these sectors than in countries such as the U.S., Canada, France and England. Finland, in particular, reports that more than one half of the country's women entrepreneurs are involved in fishing, farming and agriculture.

Types of businesses created by women also vary within countries by region (urban versus rural). Ventures owned by rural women tend to be craft, textile, and agriculturally based, whereas urban businesses more often provide clerical, hotel/restaurant, or retail sales services (Halpern, 1987, pp. 17-31).

Four factors may explain why women more often create businesses in the service sector. First, women may choose service and retail trade sectors for venture creation because they most often have knowledge, skills and prior work experience in these areas (United Nations, 1980, p. 49; van der Wees and Romjin, 1987, p. 15). A U.S. study found that occupational experience typically influences the industrial sector of the future venture of business creators (Cooper, Dunkelberg and Furuta, 1985, pp. 61-68). This is well illustrated by the country report from Great Britain that describes how former corporate secretaries have established secretarial services (Goffee and Scase, 1987). Similarly, in Japan, women business owners often transfer their domestic skills to paid self-employment by entering the hospitality industry.

Second, women typically follow courses of study in the arts or social sciences (United Nations, 1980, pp. 55-57; La Sota, 1986, pp. 24-27). For women, such skills as finance, marketing and business planning are often not learned in school. The social sciences educational background typical of women business owners can restrict or discourage them from creating or acquiring high technology, financial services, or manufacturing businesses.

Third, women often experience difficulties raising sufficient capital to start a business in capital-intensive industries. This explanation finds support in U.S. statistics: in 1982, 70.3 per cent of all women who started businesses did so with no borrowed capital (SBA, 1988,

p. 130). Possible explanations for this include gender-based discrimination in lending, women's inexperience in seeking loans, and other barriers. These obstacles will be discussed in more detail in a later section (La Sota, 1986, pp. 27-31; OECD, 1986b). Finally, women may simply prefer to be in service sector industries for a variety of personal reasons (SBA, 1988, p. 132). It is probable that some combination of all of these factors is at work.

While the industries in which women most often begin their ventures are service-oriented, the types of businesses created range from the basic to innovative (OECD, 1986b). Examples illustrative of the range of women-owned businesses include an English entrepreneur who manufactures ready-to-wear raincoats that simply offer a more neatly stitched product, to an Italian journalist who took advantage of new videotaping technology to create a unique service that tapes all television programmes and offers them to a range of corporate and public action groups.

The predominance of women-owned businesses in the service sector is consistent with general trends in industrial distribution throughout OECD countries. A variety of factors have contributed to the decline in manufacturing employment and the increase in service sector employment internationally. Estimates from the U.S. suggest that by the year 2000, nine out of every ten jobs will be generated by service sectors (SBA, 1988). This economic shift represents an opportunity for women to use skills, developed both within and outside the paid labour force, to become successfully self-employed.

However, women's enterprise creation in non-traditional sectors, such as manufacturing, is expected to increase as well. This is already occurring due to advancements in technology and communications, as well as the increasing number of women pursuing courses of study in mathematics, sciences and computers (United Nations, 1980, pp. 59-72). Recent reports from Germany and Sweden show more women starting businesses in non-traditional areas such as computer technology (OECD, 1987). The U.S. Small Business Administration notes increasing numbers of women moving into manufacturing, construction, and financial services (SBA, 1985, p. 304). A similar trend is evident in Norway where more women are starting businesses in forestry, fishing, building and construction (OECD, 1987).

Organisational Form

Although available information regarding the legal status of women-owned ventures is inconsistent across countries, it is estimated by the Centre for Research on European Women that the majority are registered as single-person businesses (CREW, 1987). Similarly, a recent European Commission study indicates that about one in six businesses run by women has the legal status of a company, with the remaining 86 per cent being classified as sole proprietorships (CREW, 1987).

In the U.S., Department of Commerce statistics show approximately 82 per cent of all women-owned businesses were classified as sole proprietorships, 8 per cent as partnerships, and 10 per cent as corporations; while for male-owned businesses, 66 per cent are sole proprietorships, 12 per cent partnerships, and 23 per cent corporations (Haber, Lamas and Lichtenstein, 1987, p. 19).

One factor that might explain the preponderance of sole proprietorships is ease of set-up (Haber, Lamas and Lichtenstein, 1987, p. 19). Other forms of business ownership have more stringent requirements at start-up, ranging from a minimum number of employees (private limited company), to constitutional formalities (incorporation), to minimum capital required (public limited company) (CREW, 1987, pp. 2-3). The costs of meeting these requirements are often not justifiable for very small or new businesses.

While no statistics are available, co-operatives as a legal form of business ownership are becoming more popular in Italy, Spain, Portugal, Turkey according to evidence presented to the European Parliament in 1989. Sectors where women's co-operatives are most popular include consumer, credit and agriculture. Co-operative ownership offers opportunities to women at start-up because it may allow for flexible work schedules, participative decision-making, pooling of business talents, and a network of social support.

Size of Business

While the growth in the number of women-owned businesses throughout OECD countries is encouraging, the size of such businesses remains small in terms of both receipts and number of employees. The European Commission study of 17 000 women reported that more than one half had no employees, one fourth employed salaried workers and 21 per cent employed family members (CREW, 1987). Similarly, a report from Great Britain indicated more than 60 per cent of self-employed women have no employees (Goffee and Scase, 1987, pp. 2-3). In Finland, 67 per cent of women-owned businesses have employees, while only 5 per cent have more than 10 (OECD, 1987). Ireland and Germany also indicate that most women-owned ventures have between 1-10 employees (O'Connor, 1987, pp. 11-12; OECD, 1987). In the U.S., Bureau of Census data indicates that in 1982 only 9.8 per cent of all women-owned businesses had employees, and of these 2.5 per cent had more than five (Gould, 1987, p. 5). Similarly, a national research study of 468 women business owners found that the majority of the respondents had between 1 and 10 employees, while 18 per cent employed 20 or more full-time employees (Hisrich and Brush, 1984, p. 34).

Size of women-owned businesses can also be measured by their revenues. While specific information on annual receipts of women-owned businesses in OECD countries is sparse, they appear to be low compared to male-owned enterprises. In 1982, the U.S. Census Bureau reported that only 11.2 per cent of all women-owned businesses had total receipts in excess of $50 000 (Gould, 1987, p. 3). The Hisrich and Brush study based on a random sample of 468 business owners also found 47 per cent of the women-owned businesses in their sample grossed less than $100 000 per year and only 16 per cent over $500 000 (Hisrich and Brush, 1984, p. 33). Other research showed that male-owned businesses in the U.S. had gross receipts three times greater than those of women business owners (La Sota, 1986, p. 88). Germany reports that female business owners have lower profits than males. Ireland notes low receipts for women business owners as well (OECD, 1987; O'Connor, 1987, pp. 11-12).

Perhaps the most logical explanation for the small size in revenues and number of employees of women-owned businesses is their young age. The astounding growth in new businesses created by women has occurred mainly in the past 5 to 7 years. Individual countries also report that the majority of women-owned businesses are less than 10 years old (U.S., Ireland and Germany, see Gould, 1987, p. 7; O'Connor, 1987, pp. 1-7; OECD, 1987). Hence, many women-owned businesses are in the early stages of the business life cycle when revenues are lower and fewer employees are required to run operations (Robinson et al., 1984, pp. 45-51). Longitudinal research in the U.S. supports this conclusion. A study of 468 women business owners over a five-year period found that established (versus new) women-owned businesses typically increased their revenues and number of employees (Hisrich and Brush, 1987, p. 194).

There is also speculation that some women business owners may deliberately maintain their businesses at a particular size out of choice, setting as primary objectives location, or control over their time, rather than maximizing growth and profits. For example, a U.S. woman business owner who owns a retail shoe business that grosses over $1 million annually says: "Although my father and brothers who are all entrepreneurs continually suggest it, I have no desire to open another store, go into mail order, relocate to a mall or expand my product line. I am happy to have control over my time and be profitable as I am."

Women business owners who deliberately maintain small-scale enterprises often find that their niche involves offering a custom service, such as interior design, or a quality hand-made craft. Many of these businesses are home-based, offering their owners a way to balance the dual responsibilities of career and family.

Evidence also shows that the educational background and occupational experience of women business owners affect the survival and growth of their ventures. Women business owners and, for that matter, all women tend to have attained a lower level of education than their male counterparts. General entrepreneurship research in the U.S. shows that there is a relationship between a higher level of education and growth of a new venture (Vesper, 1980, pp. 27-55). Similarly, U.S. studies have found a strong relationship between a higher level of education and greater profits (Begley and Boyd, 1985, p. 464), and the ability to manage cash flows effectively (Chaganti and Chaganti, 1983, p. 50).

As mentioned earlier, women usually follow courses of study in the arts or social sciences. For women who later choose business ownership, their lack of education in such subjects as finance and marketing may affect their ability to expand their enterprises. On the other hand, a liberal arts education affords women certain advantages. Effective business management requires a broad view of the organisation and strong communication skills (Vesper, 1980, pp. 49-55). Women with a liberal arts education often bring a generalist perspective to bear on their businesses, and research indicates they have strong interpersonal and organisational skills which become assets in managing a business (Hisrich and Brush, 1984, p. 35; Neider, 1987, p. 25).

Previous employment experience may also contribute to small size and limited growth of women-owned businesses. As discussed earlier, women business owners tend to have worked predominantly in the service sector. In addition, few have worked in high-level management positions or in technical fields (United Nations, 1980, p. 49). In fact, a research study in Great Britain found this to be a discriminating factor between genders: only 24 per cent of the female sample had been managers, versus 72 per cent of the male sample (Watkins and Watkins, 1983, in van der Wees and Romjin, 1987, p. 6). A report by the Small Business Association in the U.S. draws a similar conclusion, indicating that women's relative lack of work and managerial experience is one of the key differences between male and female business owners (SBA, 1988, p. 144).

This limited managerial experience means that women business owners have not had previous occupational experience in such areas as business planning, financial management, decision-making and negotiating. The lack of these skills has significant implications for both the start-up and growth of women's businesses (Timmons, 1985, pp. 179-201). Two U.S. studies found that the majority of problems encountered at start-up and in current operations lie in the area of financial planning, budgeting and managing cash flows (Hisrich and Brush, 1984, pp. 34-35; Scott, 1986, p. 42). Great Britain, France, Germany and Australia also report that weak financial skills are a problem for women business owners in venture start-up.

Finally, the level and type of prior job experience has been shown to relate to new venture growth (Vesper, 1980, pp. 27-55). There is evidence that performance is significantly enhanced and product design and development improved when the founding team has had previous upper level management experience (Chambers, Hart and Dennison, 1988, pp. 106-118). Similarly, a greater amount of prior work experience in the area of the venture has been shown to increase a business owner's chance of survival (Vesper, 1980, pp. 27-55). U.S. research reflects that the majority of women have occupational experience in the area of their venture (Hisrich and Brush, 1984, pp. 33-34; Scott, 1986, p. 39); however, there appears to be a higher percentage of women than men starting businesses in areas in which they have not had direct experience but are, instead, making a career change (van der Wees and Romjin, 1987, pp. 14-15; OECD, 1987).

Considering educational background, together with occupational experience, reveals further reason for concern about the potential for growth of women-owned businesses. A longitudinal study of U.S. women business owners exploring the relationship between "strategic origins"

Three examples of business owned by women

Self-Employed

An English woman who recognised an opportunity in the growing number of non-English speaking foreigners coming to Great Britain decided to teach English in her home. Taking no more than two students at a time, she provides lodging for them in her home and organises their leisure time. Her husband acts as administrator of the business. She has managed not only to become financially independent but to finance the conversion of her house into a comfortable residence-cum-school. Her home-based venture leaves her ample free time for other activities.

Growing Business

In 1975, a group of homemakers in the suburbs of a large Italian city were frustrated with doing undeclared paid work and not receiving credits toward retirement pension. They decided to try to become legal salaried workers using the one skill they all possessed — housework. The women set up a cleaning co-operative. By offering competent service and prices slightly lower than their competitors, they have been able to expand steadily and establish subsidiaries in other parts of Italy. Their biggest problem has been their inability to pay higher wages to employees. They feel the keys to their success have been the collective motivation of the workers (214 workers, including 24 men) and the project's financial soundness.

Grown Business

A U.S. woman founded her West Coast-based business twelve years ago with a single product and fewer than ten employees. Because she lacked a business education, the owner returned to a series of three-week sessions at a local college over three years to study subjects such as strategic planning, finance and marketing. Today the business sells micro-fiche products world wide and employs more than 70 people. The owner believes that her improved business skills and informal network of contacts have been invaluable in planning and expanding her business.

(business skills, education and occupational experience) and business growth (measured by an increase in employees and sales over a five-year period) concluded that previous occupational experience in the area of the venture, strong financial skills, and higher educational level were key factors in discriminating between growth and non-growth businesses (Brush and Hisrich, 1988).

Another factor that may influence the growth of women-owned businesses is that women's careers are frequently interrupted by marriage, childbirth or family responsibilities; for men, they are more continuous from school to training, to job, to job advancement (van der Wees and Romjin, 1987, pp. 14-15). Interruptions in career work experiences have the effect of limiting a woman's opportunity to achieve high-level management experience, which subsequently may limit her opportunity to manage and effectively develop her own business. Similarly, career interruptions may remove women from informal business networks; the resulting isolation may limit their access to information about potential customers, suppliers and sources of assistance.

Finally, growth in revenues and employees requires capital, and it is possible that many women business owners face barriers limiting their access to capital in the early stages of business growth (OECD, 1986b). These barriers will be discussed in more detail in a later section.

WOMEN AND BUSINESS OWNERSHIP: MOTIVATIONS AND APPROACHES

Motivations

"I decided to start my own business because I knew I could provide an excellent product at the right price in the marketplace."

"I was suffering too much stress from long hours as an emergency room nurse, and decided self-employment was a better option for controlling my time, especially while my two children are little."

"When I was passed over for a promotion in my company, I quit and searched for a comparable job. Unable to find one, I started my own business."

"My husband was laid off during a miners' strike and there are no other jobs in this area. Owning my own business was my only option to support my family."

These four statements suggest the range of motivations and departure points that bring women to business ownership. A woman's decision to own her own business does not usually result from a single motivating factor. For this reason, it is useful to consider the range of factors that may contribute in varying degrees to "pushing" or "pulling" a woman into business ownership (Stevenson, 1986, pp. 34-36). "Pushing" factors are defined as either personal or external forces that direct a woman towards self-employment. For instance, divorce (personal) or lay-off from a job (external) are considered push factors. Forces that "pull" a woman towards self-employment include interest in the area (personal) or market opportunity (external).

Two U.S. studies have found that push and pull forces operate together and that typically women are drawn to business ownership through a combination of job frustration and market opportunity (Hisrich and Brush, 1984, pp. 34-35; Scott, 1986, p. 41). While men are also "pushed" or "pulled" to own their own businesses, different forces affect women. Negative push factors for women include the wage gap, higher unemployment rates, and occupational segregation. Women experience additional personal push/pull factors such as the desire to get out of the house or the desire for flexible working hours to accommodate child-rearing responsibilities. For women starting a business, non-work factors, such as family, play a much stronger role than for men (Kaplan, 1988, pp. 643-653).

In addition, there is growing evidence that women's businesses pursue a range of social objectives as well as the bottom-line business objective of generating a profit. Reports from OECD countries provide examples of these social objectives: environmental protection (Italy), supplying health and nutritious food (Germany), promoting training for immigrants (Belgium), marketing products and services to women (self-defence, in England; cultural centre for women, Denmark), providing a non-traditional career option (publishing business, Wales), and taking advantage of new technological developments (synthesis images that use laser technology, France in ELISE, December 1988).

Approaches

Men and women starting their own businesses follow a similar set of steps. All new business owners must develop a product/service mix, find capital, identify and reach customers, and begin to generate income. While no statistical evidence exists regarding the particular approaches women take to accomplishing these steps, analysis of country reports, research studies and cases suggest two patterns — the evolutionary approach and the deliberate approach. Evidence suggests that the deliberate approach closely parallels the traditional business development process most often used by men, while the evolutionary approach is used by women and men with limited access to resources. The two approaches have different goals, steps and outcomes which are important to understand in developing local programme initiatives aimed specifically at women.

Deliberate Approach

The steps involved in the deliberate approach include: opportunity identification, accumulation of resources, marketing of products/services, production of products, building of the organisation and responding to society (Gartner, 1985). These steps require the ability to scan the environment in search of viable business opportunities and the technical skill to carry out a business idea (Vesper, 1980, pp. 22-55). The goal of this approach is growth; performance measures are economic, and the resulting organisation is often hierarchically structured. Businesses acquired or started in a deliberate manner tend to grow and expand quickly and are often in the financial services, manufacturing or high-technology sectors.

Women business owners using this approach generally work full-time prior to business start-up, possess up-to-date business skills and technical expertise, and have access to a network of contacts and resources. This approach is very common among young, single, educated women with significant corporate experience. Women following this approach frequently acquire, rather than create, their own businesses. They follow a deliberate, step-by-step approach that includes an active search for a market opportunity, assessment of competition, test marketing, planning and goal setting. Adequate child care and help with other domestic responsibilities are key for women following this approach because it often requires full-time work and frequent travel.

This approach is well illustrated by the example of a woman who decided to open an art gallery. She spent the first six months talking to retailers in the resort location she was considering, collecting information on housing and tourism, and contacting potential suppliers. She also prepared a business plan that projected revenues and costs over five years. A year later she opened her art gallery; the business broke even after 14 months. Eight years later she owns two galleries, is planning for a third, and has nearly doubled her revenues every year.

Women following the deliberate approach seek advice from private and public information sources. They also gather business information through informal networks with other women business owners. They are more likely to use debt or equity financing at start-up, but frequently face obstacles in locating sources of capital.

Women using the deliberate approach often encounter problems related to business growth and expansion. Lack of high-level executive experience can hinder women's attempts to expand their businesses into national and world markets. Sophisticated financial, marketing and organisational skills are needed to operate a business with multiple locations, multiple diversified product lines, or large numbers of employees. In addition, capital to fund expansion activities is frequently limited.

Evolutionary Approach

The steps involved in the evolutionary approach include: evolution of the idea, creation of a product/service using primarily personal resources, development of clientele, and maintenance of operations on a small scale. The process is relatively informal and the main considerations are customer satisfaction and the ability of the owner to maintain control over the business. The most common goal of businesses started through the evolutionary approach is to fill a niche with a unique product/service while providing an income that can support the owner and her family. Performance measures are more qualitative than in the deliberate approach; job satisfaction and goal achievement rank high in importance.

The story of a woman with a fine arts degree who sought flexible hours to be at home with her family serves as an example. One day while shopping with a friend, she came across some cotton rag rugs that she felt could be improved in colour and design. On a whim, she and her friend talked to the shop owner and subsequently arranged to design the rugs for fun. They operated the rug business as a hobby from their home for two years before deciding to set up a full-time wholesale business.

Businesses started by women in this manner have certain characteristics in common. They are created, rather than acquired or inherited. They frequently begin as an extension of a domestic skill or hobby, such as housecleaning, food preparation, sewing or hairstyling. They start slow and small, relying on personal assets for financing. Employees, if any, are subcontracted or work part-time. The business owner herself may work part-time, either out of choice or because she must juggle work and childcare responsibilities. In Norway, home-based knitting businesses are often found, while in Italy, Ireland and Spain, cottage industries in textiles and craft areas are typical.

Because these businesses evolve rather than follow formal business planning procedures, women adopting this approach need guidance in managing financial affairs and day-to-day operations, and learning basic business skills. Businesses started in the evolutionary manner frequently reach a point where the owner decides to expand and grow. In these instances, she will typically follow steps in the deliberate approach by developing a business plan (Hisrich and Brush, 1987).

Each approach requires a unique set of skills and poses a unique set of problems to the business owner. For example, in the evolutionary approach personal creativity is important, while a woman following the deliberate approach is likely to require strong financial management and marketing skills. In terms of problems, women using the evolutionary approach may find that managing operations and resolving conflicts between family and work responsibilities are particularly difficult issues, especially if the business is home-based. On the other hand, women following the deliberate approach may face difficulty in penetrating new markets, obtaining venture capital, or finding suitable full-time day care.

Enterprises initiated by low-income women

In the farming region to the south of Hamburg, Kuchen-Kate sells organic food stuffs (vegetables, fruit, milk, bread) and offers cooking lessons. Created in 1986, the business's goal is to generate new awareness among the German people about the benefits of wholefood diets. The founder, Hildegung Rabeler, started her business by renovating one of the old outbuildings on her family farm. While financial problems have hindered the business, it has benefited from community support in the form of a village renovation campaign.

Three Portuguese housewives decided to set up a business using their household knitting skills. They created their rapidly growing enterprise one step at a time. Before start-up, the three women were already making money by knitting at home while their children were young. To obtain start-up capital, they took up a collection in their neighbourhood. Despite the fact that women entrepreneurs were a rarity in their region, the three women bought a workshop and machines in 1985 with assistance from a local development initiative. Production was slow at first, but the three entrepreneurs reinvested practically all their income in the business. Today they have paid back all funds used at start-up and are seeking to network with the aim of continued growth.

Two years ago, a single 23-year-old American woman with no credit and a low-paying job decided to start her own landscaping business. She wanted to specialise in plants native to the area and use only natural insect controls and fertilizers. She was initially frustrated because her lack of credit prevented her from purchasing a truck with which to develop her business. Unable to borrow enough money for a down payment from friends and family, she solved her problem by applying for a credit card, borrowing the down payment on the credit card, and financing the truck from the dealer. Next, she worked with a professional consultant to assess the market, determine her target customers and prepare cash flows. Today her business is thriving; she has five full-time employees, and was recently recognised as business woman of the year for her local area.

BARRIERS FACED BY WOMEN BUSINESS OWNERS

"Women are no different than men in their entrepreneurial drive and their desire for the economic independence and self-fulfillment that business ownership can bring. However, there is a catch — it tends to be more difficult for women to live out this drive" (Charlotte Taylor, *Women and the Business Game*).

When a business is created, obtaining adequate resources, dealing with formidable government regulations and taxes, successfully reaching or creating a market, and structuring the business and its relationships within an industry are common challenges for all entrepreneurs. Dealing with them requires confidence, hard work, information and resources. Research shows, however, that in most Western countries women business owners face particular barriers to successful business ownership related to their status in society, access to information, and access to capital resources. Recognising that these barriers will vary in level and intensity by country, industry, and the experiences of the individual woman business owner, it is only possible to offer a general description and discuss their implications.

Women's Status

Although women business owners enjoy greater visibility than at any previous time, their efforts are hindered by their overall status in society. This status is influenced heavily by historical assumptions that a women's primary responsibility is to care for her home and children. Such assumptions have led to a range of prevailing negative attitudes about and towards women who choose to — or because of economic circumstances must — enter the paid labour force.

Gender-based expectations of women and the attitude that women should not work, let alone own and operate a business, lower the credibility of many women business owners. One study in the U.S. revealed that women starting new businesses face difficulty in overcoming society's beliefs that they "are not as serious as men about business" (Hisrich and O'Brien, 1982). Another U.S. study found that women business owners were brought up by their parents to believe men are more important and a woman's ultimate role in life is to be a wife and mother (Stevenson, 1984). The barriers posed by attitudes such as these are particularly high for women attempting business start-up in non-traditional industries and for low-income and minority women.

In addition, public laws, government regulations, and institutional policies have reinforced socio-cultural norms and attitudes. Some countries have discouraged dual wage-earner families through tax policy, while others have restricted the occupations a woman can enter, her degree of ownership in a business, or her ability to join a trade union. Similarly, most countries lack adequate and affordable childcare options.

As a result of this legacy, women desiring to own and operate a business have few role models. The successful business owner is almost always portrayed as a white man and most business literature reinforces this stereotype. This, in turn, reinforces women's lack of confidence in their ability to successfully start a venture (OECD, 1986b).

Access to Information and Assistance

All new and inexperienced business owners have difficulty making their way through the maze of formal business support organisations to locate reliable information and assistance. For women, however, locating a source of assistance does not always solve the problem. The attitudes of many training and technical assistance providers frequently reinforce women's negative self-image in the business arena because they often dismiss women's business activities as "hobbies" and generally fail to recognise that special approaches are needed to assist different kinds of women (Gould, 1987, p. 17).

Information needs of women business owners will vary depending on their previous occupational/educational experience, location and type of business. Women who were not in the paid labour force prior to venture creation will need general business information and opportunities to meet others in business, while women working full-time may need technical assistance in a specific area of business operation. Similarly, rural women business owners may have greater difficulty in gaining access to information about markets and financing, while urban women business owners may require assistance in analysing the competition.

Finally, the type of information needed by women business owners will depend on the type of business they are starting. For example, a French woman business owner starting a laser technology business required cutting edge information on scientific imaging, as well as assistance in accomplishing a comprehensive market research study. On the other hand, ten Irish housewives needed financial information and training in general business skills before opening their Dublin restaurant (ELISE, 1988).

Women operating or starting up a small business are very often excluded from informal networks of information such as male-only clubs, old boy networks, and business lunches. This represents a significant barrier because research shows that strong ties in social networks are not only an advantage for obtaining information, but actually facilitate the entire business start-up process (Aldrich, Rosen and Woodward, 1987, pp. 167-168). Further, informal networks are more important in business creation than formal networks (Birley, 1985, p. 336). Such informal information exchange processes can be critical to locating suppliers, employees, and customers (La Sota, 1986, pp. 29-30). Women starting up their businesses part-time while continuing their domestic responsibilities may suffer a degree of isolation that especially limits their opportunities to develop business contacts. Similarly, many women of colour face even greater obstacles in developing ties or entering networks due to racial discrimination.

Access to Capital

All business owners face a barrier in obtaining sufficient and affordable capital to start or acquire a venture. Most start-ups, in fact, are financed by personal assets and savings. Women business owners who decide to seek outside financing, however, face greater difficulties than men because of their lack of credibility, the type and relatively small scale of their business endeavours, and their lack of experience in negotiating financial matters.

A lack of credibility in the economic area is nowhere more evident than when a woman tries to borrow money. Whether she seeks financing from her spouse, another family member or friend, or a conventional lender, any woman is likely to encounter an assumption — intensified for low-income women and women of colour — that women cannot manage money successfully (Gould, 1987, p. 17). Moreover, men in the financial community often perceive women to be poorer business risks because of possible household and family responsibilities, especially when the customer is a single parent. If a woman business owner does not have a credit history in her own name, has a poor credit history, or if she is a low-income woman, a co-signer may be required to obtain a loan (Halpern, 1987, pp. 127-128). The perception still exists in some countries that women lack business qualities and, therefore, are greater financial risks than men (OECD, 1986b). This perception runs counter to the evidence.

The type and relatively small scale of many women's businesses make it difficult to meet the minimum loan size and collateral requirements of most conventional lenders. Women are less likely than men to own personal assets outright, or to control shared assets, such as a house or car, which can be used as collateral (Sexton and Bowman-Upton, 1988). Similarly, as a result of the predominantly service-oriented work experiences of women, they are less likely to start manufacturing or other kinds of businesses with fixed assets that can serve as collateral.

In addition, most women-owned businesses require a relatively small amount of capital, usually far less than $50 000 at start-up (Halpern, 1987, pp. 127-128). The U.S. reports that often women start their ventures with under $11 000, which represents approximately half the amount used by men (SBA, 1988, p. 132). Conventional lenders usually shun such small amounts, due primarily to their high transaction and information costs (Halpern, 1987, pp. 127-128).

Finally, women business owners lack business experience in negotiating financial matters. They are often uncertain about how to present their case to obtain capital and frequently lack confidence in approaching potential formal and informal lenders and investors (OECD, 1986b). It may be the case that women business owners distrust financial institutions and will save personal funds, waiting longer to start up rather than seeking institutional support (Halpern, 1987, p. 128).

NATIONAL POLICIES TOWARDS WOMEN'S BUSINESS OWNERSHIP

Many OECD countries have designed and implemented policies to promote enterprise creation by women[4]. These policies aim mainly at lessening unemployment by tapping existing local resources. The scope, focus and success in implementation of these policies varies widely across OECD countries.

The Nordic countries have enacted policies favourable to women business owners. In Sweden, policies benefit entrepreneurs in general, while special arrangements and support encourage enterprise development by women. Women have learned about self-employment opportunities through two national trade fairs and a series of seminars. In addition, the Swedish Regional Development Fund now arranges women-only courses and offers start-up grants to women-owned businesses.

Similarly, Norway encourages the creation of women-owned businesses through its Small Business Development Project that provides both loans and training. In Finland, start-up allowances enable women to establish businesses as well. In Spain, the National Institute of Women, with ten offices across the country, encourages women to start up in business and organises training courses to support them. Turkey promotes small-scale industry for women, particularly in areas such as textiles and clothing.

In Australia, the New Enterprise Incentive Scheme targets unemployed workers and, specifically, unemployed women. In addition, a National Advisory Group on Local Employment Initiatives is collecting information on women-owned businesses to assist in designing future public policies.

While the general economic programme of the Netherlands promotes entrepreneurial activity, the country also recognises women's special barriers to obtaining financial backing and offers an experimental scheme of financial assistance. France encourages women to play a larger role in the economy through the co-ordinated efforts of the Ministry of Women's Rights and the Ministry of Labour. Job creation schemes have also been implemented; the Ministry of Women's Rights assisted in launching 65 firms between 1981 and 1984 by funding training and providing direct financial support. Canada also promotes a positive approach to women's business ownership through its Department of Female Entrepreneurship, whose task it is to increase the visibility of women-owned businesses and encourage women to enter business life.

In some countries, women business owners can gain access to public financial backing. In Germany, between 1980 and 1986, nearly one quarter of public-sector loans to business creators were made to women (Schmelcher, 1987, p. 19). German women have also been able to take advantage of general programmes sponsored by the Ministry of Labour which offer rent subsidies and financing. However, no programmes specifically target the training or financial needs of women business owners (Schmelcher, 1987, pp. 2-3).

In Great Britain, public policy encourages women to take advantage of assistance available to small businesses. A joint study conducted by the Department of Employment and Shell U.K.

attempted to identify the specific barriers encountered by women attempting business ownership (Goffee and Scase, 1987). Part of this programme is implemented through the Scottish Enterprise Foundation which has the dual mission of conducting research to determine the problems and needs of women business owners, and providing gender-specific training that emphasizes active learning and skill building (Rosa, 1988, p. 2; Hartshorn and Richardson, 1988, p. 16). Other schemes which women may use for assistance in business creation include an Enterprise Allowance Scheme that enables unemployed people to attempt self-employment, the Department of Employment's small firm counselling service, and guaranteed loans for small firms (Goffee and Scase, 1987, pp. 19-20).

The job creation policies and programmes of Austria and Finland promote and subsidise self-administered enterprises by unemployed persons, but are not specifically directed at women.

Finally, the development of entrepreneurship and self-employment among women has been supported by the Women's Bureau of the U.S. Department of Labor, as an option for some women seeking a niche in the labour market. Programmes to assist women who wish to become entrepreneurs, however, are under the jurisdiction of the U.S. Small Business Administration, an independent agency. Training programmes for women have been developed in most of the local area Small Business Development Centers around the country. Usually they are conducted through local colleges and universities. They range from classes in how to get started and thinking through a business concept, to management skills and how to expand a growing business.

In October 1988, the U.S. Congress passed the Women's Business Ownership Act of 1988. The bill provides funds for the establishment of public/private demonstration projects to provide training and management assistance to women business owners, amends the Equal Credit Opportunity Act of 1974 to require banks to give written explanation for loan denial, creates a special Small Business Administration guaranteed mini-loan programme for amounts up to $50 000, and promotes greater access to federal procurement for women's businesses.

Despite these generally favourable national policies towards women's enterprise development, experience indicates that assistance programmes may not reach more than 5 per cent of the target group (van der Wees and Romjin, 1987, p. 30). This may occur because, although governments aim to develop measures and opportunities which benefit men and women equally, women face greater barriers in developing and managing a business (OECD, 1986b). For this reason, blanket policies will not always work. Special attention is needed in specific areas on both national and local levels to encourage growth and development of women-owned businesses.

CONCLUSION

The growth in the number of women-owned businesses is expected to continue in all OECD countries as a result of women's increasing interest in entrepreneurship, greater government attention to, and encouragement of, women-owned businesses, and a growing acceptance of women as business owners due to their increasing numbers and the impact of their businesses as measured by job creation, technological innovation, and material and services contributions to society. In addition, a greater number of women business owners will enter non-traditional sectors of activity.

Many countries suffer trade deficits, budget difficulties, and decreased productivity, challenging public policy-makers to catalyse the pool of talent represented by women business owners. However, a greater awareness of the obstacles faced by women in obtaining information, accessing capital and overcoming negative attitudes is needed in all OECD countries so that new women-owned businesses can survive and existing ones can prosper. Further, recognising the diverse needs of women business owners — depending on industry sector, approach taken to venture creation, regional location, and occupational and educational experience — is crucial.

The majority of women-owned businesses are young and have not yet reached the mature stage in business development. It is expected that women-owned businesses will grow in size and scope, contributing to local economies in revenues, jobs, goods and services.

NOTES

1. Statistics are collected by different agencies in OECD countries and a variety of terms are used but definitions are seldom made explicit.

   Australia: Labour Force surveys and the Census of Population measure the number of self-employed and employers.

   Austria: the Federal Ministry of Labour and Social Affairs collects data on the number of women self-employed.

   Belgium and **Denmark** both keep track of independently employed women.

   Finland keeps track of the number of female self-employed and employers in the Finnish Population Census. A combination of the two statistics is counted as the number of female entrepreneurs.

   France: National agencies keep track of employers and new business creators.

   Germany: female entrepreneurs are women who establish businesses on their own; statistics for self-employed people are maintained by the government.

   Great Britain: Labour Force Surveys and the Office of Population Censuses and Surveys maintain statistics on the numbers of self-employed females and employers. Independent business proprietors are not distinguished by gender.

   Greece counts female employers and those who work for themselves.

   The Netherlands refers to self-employed as those who start new businesses or small-scale businesses and statistics are collected by the Ministry of Social Affairs.

   Norway: Labour Market statistics keep track of new entrepreneurship (new businesses registered) by gender.

   Sweden uses the term "entrepreneurs" to mean new businesses created.

   United States: Three government agencies keep track of different statistics — Census Bureau counts women-owned small businesses, the Bureau of Labor Statistics keeps track of self-employed females, and the Internal Revenue Service (IRS) keeps track of female employers. The discrepancies in definitions, interpretation of terms, and inconsistent availability of data creates difficulties in accurately identifying the number of female business creators and owners. A statement in the United States Report on Small Business supports this: "There is no total count of female-operated businesses in the U.S." (SBA, 1985, p. 295). The Internal Revenue Service and the Bureau of Census collect different information, and the SBA estimates the number of businesses operated by women based on a combination of this data.

2. "Self-employed" is conventionally defined as "owners of unincorporated businesses", *OECD Employment Outlook 1986*, p. 43.

3. Unless otherwise indicated, data are drawn from the papers and country reports prepared for the OECD Conference on Women — Local Initiatives — Job Creation held in Oslo in May 1987 (OECD, 1987).

4. See the country reports, etc., in OECD (1987).

REFERENCES

Aldrich, Howard, Ben Rosen and William Woodward (1987) "The Impact of Social Networks on Business Foundings and Profit", in *Frontiers of Entrepreneurial Research*, Center for Entrepreneurial Studies, Babson College, Wellesley, Mass., pp. 154-168.

Begley, Thomas M. and David P. Boyd (1985) "Company and Chief Executive Officer Characteristics Related to Financial Performance in Smaller Businesses", in *Frontiers of Entrepreneurial Research*, ed. J.A. Hornaday *et al.*, Center for Entrepreneurial Studies, Babson College, Wellesley, Mass., pp. 453-467.

Birley, Sue (1985) "The Role of Networks in the Entrepreneurial Process", in *Frontiers of Entrepreneurial Research*, Center for Entrepreneurial Studies, Babson College, Wellesley, Mass., pp. 325-337.

Brush, Candida G. and Robert Hisrich (1988) "The Woman Entrepreneur: Strategic Origins: Impact on Growth", in *Frontiers of Entrepreneurial Research*, Center for Entrepreneurial Studies, Babson College, Wellesley, Mass., pp. 612-625.

Chaganti, Rajeswarao and Radharao Chaganti (1983) "A Profile of Profitable and Not So Profitable Businesses", *Journal of Small Business Management*, 21(3), pp. 43-51.

Chambers, Brian, Stuart Hart and Daniel Dennison (1988) "Founding Team Experience and New Firm Performance", in *Frontiers of Entrepreneurial Research*, Center for Entrepreneurial Studies, Babson College, Wellesley, Mass., pp. 106-118.

Cooper, Arnold, William C. Dunkelberg and Stanley Furuta (1985) "Incubator Organisations — Background and Founding Characteristics", in *Frontiers of Entrepreneurial Research*, Center for Entrepreneurial Studies, Babson College, Wellesley, Mass., pp. 61-67.

CREW (Center for Research on European Women) (1987) *"Women's Businesses: Legal, Administrative and Financial Environment — Some Examples"*, Brussels.

ELISE (1988) "Women in Business: A Career as an Entrepreneur, 20 Project Profiles", Local Employment Initiatives in Europe, Information Network, December.

Gartner, William B. (1985) *"Conceptual Framework for Describing the Phenomenon of New Venture Creation"*, Academy of Management Review, 10(4), pp. 696-706.

Goffee, Robert and Richard Scase (1985) *Women in Charge: The Experience of the Female Entrepreneur*, Allen & Unwin, London.

Goffee, Robert and Richard Scase (1987) *"Patterns of Female Entrepreneurship in Britain"*, OECD, Paris, May.

Gould, Sara K. (1987) *"Report of the National Strategy Session on Women's Self-Employment"*, Corporation for Enterprise Development, Washington, D.C., May.

Haber, Sheldon, Enrique Lamas and Jules H. Lichtenstein (1987) "On Their Own: The self employed and others in private business", *Monthly Labour Review*, May, pp. 20-27.

Halpern, Monique (1987) "Business Creation By Women: Motivation, Situation, and Perspectives — Final Report of a Study for the E.E.C.", September.

Hartshorn, C. and P. Richardson (1988) "The Role of Gender Specific Training in Helping Women Survive in the Establishment of a Business", Scottish Enterprise Foundation, *Conference Paper Series No. 37/88*, November.

Hisrich, Robert D. and Candida G. Brush (1983) "The Woman Entrepreneur: Implications of Family, Education and Occupational Experience", in *Frontiers of Entrepreneurial Research*, Center for Entrepreneurial Studies, Babson College, Wellesley, Mass., pp. 255-270.

Hisrich, Robert D. and Candida G. Brush (1984) "The Woman Entrepreneur: Management Skills and business problems", *Journal of Small Business Management*, 22(1), pp. 30-38.

Hisrich, Robert D. and Candida G. Brush (1987) "The Woman Entrepreneur: A Longitudinal Study", in *Frontiers of Entrepreneurial Research*, Center for Entrepreneurial Studies, Babson College, Wellesley, Mass., pp. 187-189.

Hisrich, Robert D., and Marie O'Brien (1982) "The Woman Entrepreneur as a Reflection of the Type of Business", *Frontiers of Entrepreneurial Research*, Center for Entrepreneurial Studies, Babson College, Wellesley, Mass., pp. 54-77.

Kaplan, Eileen (1988) "Women Entrepreneurs: Constructing a Framework to Examine Venture Success and Business Failure", in *Frontiers of Entrepreneurial Research*, Center for Entrepreneurial Studies, Babson College, Wellesley, Mass..

La Sota, Marcia (ed.) (1986) *Women and Business Ownership — A Bibliography*, Minnesota Scholarly Press, Inc., Mankato, Minn.

Neider, Linda (1987) "A Preliminary Investigation of Female Entrepreneurs in Florida", *Journal of Small Business Management*, 25(3), pp. 22-29.

O'Connor, Joyce (1987) *Women in Enterprise*, Industrial Development Authority and Office of Minister of State for Women's Affairs, Dublin.

OECD (1986) "Local Initiatives for Employment Creation", *ILE Notebook* No. 6, Paris.

OECD (1987) Issues papers and country reports prepared for the Conference on "Women — Local Initiatives — Job Creation" held in Oslo, May.

Robinson, Richard B., John A. Pearce II, George A. Vozikis and Timothy Mescon (1984) "The Relationship between Stage of Development and Small Firm Planning and Performance", *Journal of Small Business Management*, 22(2), pp. 45-52.

Rosa, Peter (1988) *"Research in the Scottish Enterprise Foundation"*, Scottish Enterprise Foundation, May.

SBA (U.S. Small Business Administration) (1985) *Report of the President on Small Business*, U.S. Government Printing Office, Washington, D.C.

SBA (U.S. Small Business Administration)(1988) *Small Business in the American Economy*, U.S. Government Printing Office, Washington, D.C.

Schmelcher, Ingrid (1987) "The 'Markthalle' — A Model of Support for Women Entrepreneurs", OECD, Paris, May.

Scott, Carol E. (1986) "Why More Women are Becoming Entrepreneurs, *Journal of Small Business Management*, 24(4), pp. 37-44.

Sexton, Donald and Nancy Bowman-Upton (1988) "Sexual Stereotyping of Female Entrepreneurs: A Comparative Psychological Trait Analysis of Female and Male Entrepreneurs", in *Frontiers of Entrepreneurial Research*, Center for Entrepreneurial Studies, Babson College, Wellesley, Mass., pp. 654-655.

Silvestri, George and John Lucasiewiecz (1987) "A Look at Occupational Employment Trends to the Year 2000", *Monthly Labour Review*, September, pp. 46-63.

Stevenson, Lois (1986) "Against All Odds: The Entrepreneurship of Women", *Journal of Small Business Management*, 24(4), pp. 30-36.

Timmons, Jeffry A. (1985) *New Venture Creation*, 2nd edn, Richard D. Irwin, Inc., Homewood, Ill.

United Nations (1980) *The Economic Role of Women in the EEC Region*, United Nations, New York.

van der Wees, Catherine and Henny Romjin (1987) *"Entrepreneurship and Small Enterprise Development for Women in Developing Countries: An Agenda of Unanswered Questions"*, International Labour Organisation, Geneva.

Vesper, Karl H. (1980) *New Venture Strategies*, Prentice Hall Inc., Englewood Cliffs, New Jersey.

LOCAL RESPONSES: WHAT IS AND WHAT COULD BE

Given the important role of women in local enterprise creation, it is in the interest of communities (and countries) to accept the challenge of assisting women to release their full entrepreneurial potential. The chapters of Part II present strategies for assisting women to become self-employed or expand their self-employment businesses.

Chapter IV examines a range of intermediary organisations and programmes that assist both self-employed women and women with an active interest in business ownership. Chapter V examines the issues faced by self-employed women who wish to expand their businesses, and offers insights into development programmes that can effectively assist growing businesses. Finally, Chapter VI presents some conclusions and recommendations, and outlines a framework for local implementation and action.

The focus of Part II is on businesses where the original purpose is self-employment, rather than dramatic growth. Women who follow growth-company strategies are more likely to be adequately served by existing business programmes. In addition, most of the public-sector support for women entrepreneurs in the OECD countries is directed at self-employment programmes.

Chapter IV

THE ROLE OF INTERMEDIARIES
IN STRENGTHENING WOMEN'S SELF-EMPLOYMENT ACTIVITIES

Chris Weiss

INTRODUCTION

In West Virginia, in the United States, Shirley wants to buy a stamping machine to expand her rubber stamp production business. In Barcelona, Josefa tries to learn how to put together a business plan. In Birmingham, England, Jane is recently unemployed and wants to find out how to start a business under the Enterprise Allowance Scheme. In Paris, Marie-Claire is ready to expand her successful restaurant and wonders where to borrow the money. What do these women have in common? They can all benefit from the services of intermediaries, organisations in the public or private sector that provide services to women (and sometimes men) to help them start or expand their businesses.

This chapter will illustrate the role that intermediary organisations and programmes can play in strengthening women's self-employment activities. It begins with a look at the purposes and overall goals of intermediaries, and then describes a range of programme approaches in the areas of training, technical assistance and financing. It then addresses how new intermediary programmes and organisations are started, and concludes by examining the question of funding for programme development and operation.

PURPOSES AND OVERALL GOALS OF INTERMEDIARIES

An intermediary organisation or programme provides the link that is often necessary between a woman's dream and a viable, job-creating venture. Intermediaries intervene in the business development process by providing assistance — in the form of training, technical assistance and/or financing — to women to increase the likelihood that their entrepreneurial efforts will succeed.

Intermediaries take different forms in different countries, depending on the culture, political climate and, to a certain extent, the strength of the women's movement and the degree to which women have raised their economic concerns to a policy level. In communities in Denmark, the Netherlands and Norway, for example, the public sector has functioned as an intermediary by operating programmes to train women in small business development. In other communities in the

59

United States, the United Kingdom and Germany, women themselves have gathered resources from both the public and the private sectors to form new private-sector organisations that act as advocates for female entrepreneurs. And, in localities in many countries, existing public or private business development organisations have augmented their services by designing new business development programmes focused on women.

Existing intermediaries describe their missions in several different ways. The Women's Enterprise Development Agency in the United Kingdom, for example, has as its purpose to "assist women to create a living for themselves through enterprise" (Women's Enterprise Development Agency, 1986, p. 10). In Germany, the Frauenbetriebe describes its mission as women helping other women to learn "where the highest hurdles are in order to jump over them" (Haas, 1987, p. 8). In the United States, the Women's Economic Development Corporation (WEDCO) assists women to "become self-sufficient through self-employment".

Women's Enterprise Development Agency

The Women's Enterprise Development Agency (WEDA) assists women in creating a living for themselves through enterprise. WEDA targets its services to low-income and minority women. Its origins are found in the Women and Work Programme of the Aston University Management Centre. Jane Skinner and Olwyn Cupid served as the first co-directors; of the 350 different enterprise agencies in Britain, WEDA is one of only five headed by women.

WEDA works to:

— *Identify, support and assist individual women/groups of women who are interested in self-employment and starting businesses;*

— *Encourage "new" modes of business and self-employment to emerge, run by women;*

— *Act as a central agency for specialised assistance to women's enterprises in all fields; it also acts as a referral agency to other business advisory services;*

— *Improve women's access to finance for business purposes;*

— *Encourage better understanding between existing advisory/financial institutions and women, in the interest of women's business development. This involves, in particular, helping to change traditional attitudes;*

— *Conduct research into women's involvement in business — to learn why and how women start businesses and to help design effective training/support programmes.*

Located in Birmingham, WEDA has assisted in the start-up of other women's enterprise development agencies.

Designing and implementing enterprise development strategies that benefit women is a relatively new activity in all of the OECD countries. Practitioners in the field are at the stage of clarifying their goals and experimenting with various methods to learn what works and what does not. The majority of intermediaries, however, pursue one or more of the following overall goals:

1. Increasing the number of jobs at income levels that enable women to support themselves and their families;
2. Increasing business ownership by women;
3. Empowering women through the creation of challenging and satisfying work and increased participation in workplace decision-making; and
4. Broadening the employment and income-generating options available to unemployed and underemployed women.

New intermediary organisations in the United States have put strong emphasis on the fourth goal, that of broadening the economic options available to lower-income women, as a means to alleviate poverty. This is not the case in most other OECD countries, where programmes typically do not place any special focus on assisting low-income women.

Approaches taken by Intermediaries

Intermediary organisations in the OECD countries can be grouped into three general categories lying along a continuum. Organisations in the first category offer primarily training courses in small business development to women. Often, this emphasis on training results from a needs assessment process that reveals that women have different learning requirements from men, particularly in relation to business start-up. Organisations in the second category combine training courses with other services for female entrepreneurs, mainly access to credit and, in some cases, access to low-cost space in business incubators. Organisations in the third category view entrepreneurship as part of an economic development process and, as a result, concentrate on advocacy and other activities that aim to create a public policy environment which fosters and promotes women's business development efforts. In each category, some intermediaries run programmes aimed at women only, while others offer programmes open to both men and women.

An important characteristic shared by intermediaries in all three categories is an emphasis on partnership. Programme operators learn quickly that collaboration with a wide variety of actors in both the public and private sectors is the key to achieving their goals and objectives. The benefit to women is greatest when intermediaries reach out to, and make effective use of, the range of resources and skills found within any community or region.

Training to Strengthen Small Business Development Efforts

Most intermediaries offer entrepreneurial training in some form. Such training assists women to accomplish those tasks that lead to successful business start-up: developing a business plan, learning business-related language, sharpening decision-making and personal effectiveness skills, and learning systems, such as recordkeeping, that are crucial to setting up business operations.

Entrepreneurial training is typically offered either in the classroom or through individual consulting, although a single programme may combine elements of both approaches. Under a classroom training model, women attend a series of sessions held over a 12-20 week period. Classroom training programmes use various instructional techniques, such as lectures, resource speakers, group exercises and case studies. Classroom training may be followed by a period of individual consulting as women start their business activities.

Under an individual consulting model, women work one-to-one with professional consultants to develop the business plan and discuss issues related to business start-up. Business plan preparation is often accomplished as clients complete a series of "homework" assignments to which the consultant reacts with feedback and suggestions for revisions. In addition, small groups may be formed to meet on a short-term basis to address common start-up problems and to offer mutual support.

Both classroom-based and individual consulting programmes rely heavily on women's own motivation to complete assignments and move forward towards business start-up. Women who are not highly motivated soon drop out, reducing the need for programmes to use scarce resources in costly, up-front screening activities.

As regards charging fees for training services, intermediaries in different countries take different approaches. Most European programmes do not charge a fee for their services, while programmes in the United States often do. Programme operators point out that paying for services reinforces the notion that women are making an investment in the training and establishes a business-like relationship between trainer and trainee. When fees are charged, however, a sliding scale is often used to index the fee paid to a woman's income level.

A partnership operated by the Technological Institute in Storstroms County in Denmark and the county's Labour Market Office provides an example of a training-focused intermediary programme (Storstroms LMO, 1987, pp. 1-11). Storstroms County, located south of Copenhagen, has concentrated for the past several years on entrepreneurship training for men and women as part of its effort to combat unemployment. In 1987, five women from the Institute designed a course for women only, patterned after recent experience in Norway that demonstrated a positive response to women-only courses. According to a paper describing the nordic experience with women's businesses, "In general, women entrepreneurs express the view that they find it problematic to start a new business. They experience a lack of self-confidence and information, obstacles which are also evident in other countries. Therefore, women often prefer women-only courses and support. They say that they feel more free to talk and less worried about showing their ignorance if they are among women only" (Wickmann and Sundin, 1987, p. 3).

The Institute's course includes 70 hours of training over a four-month period. Classes are held from late afternoon Friday to late afternoon Saturday to accommodate women who work outside the home or who have family responsibilities. There is a three-week interval between classes and participants must complete homework assignments before returning to the next session. The course combines teaching, group experience and peer exchange, and is restricted to women over the age of 25.

The Institute conducted an evaluation following the pilot course in the spring of 1987 (Bottrup, 1988, pp. 1-55). Twenty-four women enrolled in the pilot course, recruited from a group of approximately 80 women, and all but one completed the course. Overall, participants rated the course as very effective on a survey that was taken three months after course completion. The evaluation found that the course was most effective for those who were ready to start a business immediately or had started a short time before enrolment. It was least effective for those who lacked a business idea or had been in business for a while. Of the 23 women who finished, four were in business when they started, three started businesses at the end of the course, and the remainder were in various stages of start-up. A few had secured better jobs as a result of the training.

The course was run again in Storstroms County during the fall of 1987 and the spring of 1988. Almost half of the county's budget for this activity is targeted to women entrepreneurs. According to a publication about their programmes, the county's rationale is that women should account for a larger share of total entrepreneurs. Currently, only 15 per cent of the county's entrepreneurs are women, and "future figures show that during the next ten years the region will have a decrease within the male labour force, but a continuing increase within the female force" (Storstroms LMO,

1987, p. 6). Clearly the county is looking ahead and targeting women, upgrading their skills for job creation activities.

The Danish experience is echoed in other OECD countries. A similar programme, but with a slightly different focus, operates in Barcelona, Spain under the sponsorship of the city government. According to Mrs. Josefa Sanchez, the Centre d'Autoocupacio de la Dona operates a 16-week programme for groups of 15 young women from the ages of 18 to 25. Benefiting from an international exchange with the Women's Economic Development Corporation in St. Paul, Minnesota, in 1986, the Barcelona programme designed a pre-screening process to select participants. The process tests for tolerance of risk and ability to set priorities, and includes a personal interview. The Centre intends to expand its services by operating a credit programme and targeting business opportunities that are not traditional for women.

Yet another programme of this type, the Alida de Jong School, operates in Utrecht, the Netherlands (van der Meer, 1986). The school is an initiative of the women's union, FNV, which is open to all women and affiliated with the Netherlands' trade union federation. The school operates a course in business start-up for individuals or groups of women wanting to start collectives. The course involves two to three days of training each week for about ten months and is targeted to women returning to work after a number of years at home (see box).

Alida de Jong School

"The Alida de Jong School in the Netherlands occupies a special place among the institutions providing courses for women. The School has developed a business course for women aged over 25 and with a low level of education who have clearly thought-out plans for a business of their own.

It is the only course covered by our survey where participation is subject to any such restriction. The School teaches its students how to develop systematic plans for the establishment of their businesses and how to run them once they are established. All practical subjects are taught and students' self-confidence is strengthened through training in social skills. (The course lasts ten months 2 1/2 days/week). A creche is provided, with qualified nursery assistant, for children aged 1-4; participants are asked to make a small payment if they wish to make use of it."

Source: Leni van der Meer, Survey of women entrepreneurs and support organisations in the Netherlands conducted under the auspices of the European Centre for the Development of Vocational Training, September 1988.

At the seminar on Women — Local Initiatives — Job Creation held in Oslo in 1987, participants in a workshop on "Support and Training" agreed that the incidence of business failure could be lowered with well-designed training programmes. "Training, guidance and advice were considered extremely important for the woman-entrepreneur to be able to survive. Without this support a 60 per cent failure rate could be expected after four years. With training and support this could be reduced to 12 per cent and with after-care, even to 2 per cent" (OECD, 1987b). While it is not known how reliable these figures are, all training programmes report a better record of successful business start-up for their participants than for women who start without the benefit of such training.

Training Women in Co-operative Development

Training programme representatives participating in the Oslo meeting also agreed that working with groups of women starting a co-operative activity differed in a few key respects from working with sole proprietors. Whereas individual women often benefit from training and support in personal effectiveness skills, co-operatives need training in group decision-making techniques and methods to promote shared leadership.

In many OECD countries, intermediaries work with groups of rural women with handcraft skills who have joined together to generate income from their craft-related activities. At the Oslo conference, Elizabeth de Jong of the Selbu Home Crafts Centre in Norway, described the Centre's work with a group of knitters. The group started up when elderly women began to teach younger women to knit gloves and sweaters in traditional Norwegian patterns, a dying craft in rural Norway. They formed a co-operative, and the Centre assists them in creating new designs for a contemporary market and adapting the old handknitting techniques to knitting machines. Their success in marketing has led them to reach out to other co-operatives for help in meeting growing production levels.

Ms. de Jong drew some conclusions from the women's success, she emphasized their common cultural background, financial and technical support from municipal authorities, local media coverage, and a commitment to the project by the women involved. Similar conditions exist in West Virginia (U.S.), where an intermediary called Women and Employment, Inc. has extensive experience working with craft co-operatives, including one producing traditional Appalachian quilts. Trainers in West Virginia have developed a curriculum that includes specific tasks for women to accomplish as a group, including training in conflict resolution.

Training Women in Non-traditional Industries

Many programmes offer special assistance to women pursuing business start-up or expansion in non-traditional industry sectors. Intermediaries in Norway, Spain, West Virginia, the Netherlands and elsewhere target special support to women running companies in the manufacturing, construction, finance, or high technology sectors. In the Netherlands, priority in financing is given to those businesses in which women will work in a traditional male occupation. In Norway, using the model of equal employment opportunity programmes developed in the U.S. in the late 1970s, officials have targeted affirmative action resources to the county which serves as the centre of oil-related activities.

Financing and Other Services in Support of Enterprise Creation

Many intermediaries in OECD countries offer services in addition to training. Depending on several factors, including the availability of funding, these groups incorporate financing, low-cost space, assistance in meeting personal needs, and public policy remedies, including overcoming transfer payment programme barriers, into their programme offerings. By assuming such an expanded role; an intermediary's involvement in active and vocal advocacy activities on behalf of women entrepreneurs often increases.

The component most frequently added to training curricula is access to credit. Women around the world request assistance in gaining access to capital. The following quote from a study conducted by the Equal Opportunities Council in the Netherlands may describe the experience of women in all OECD countries:

"At the pre-establishment stage the main obstacles lie in the area of finance... women have greater difficulty than men in obtaining credit, whether from the banks or from the state, for the creation of a business. This is due to their supposed lack of credit worthiness.... The problem is compounded by the fact that credit advisors, who are almost all men, are not generally acquainted with any examples of successful women entrepreneurs. Against this background the judgments reached regarding women's business plans are more often subjective than in the case of those put forward by men" (van der Meer, 1986, p. 33).

Many intermediaries in OECD countries have recognised the barrier posed by lack of access to credit and designed various schemes to overcome it. Such schemes include revolving loan funds, group lending mechanisms, and establishing new relationships with conventional lenders through loan guarantee programmes and initial screening of prospective clients.

In Minnesota, the Women's Economic Development Corporation (WEDCO) created a $1.2 million loan fund that makes short-term loans ranging in size from $200 to $15 000 to clients who have been refused credit by a conventional lender. Loans can be made in the form of direct, outright loans, guarantees, or lines of credit drawn down on a pre-arranged schedule. A loan fund committee decides on the type, amount and terms of each loan. According to WEDCO:

"In situations where we are worried about a new business owner and her potential to repay the debt and make the business work, we often provide a smaller loan to test both the concept and the owner. We call this process stepping and will loan a smaller amount of money in order to produce the product and make a sale. If this is successful, and the amount is repaid, we will then loan a second amount. In this situation we have been very successful in providing an incentive for the business owner, a fairly low risk situation for both parties, and creating opportunities that are win-win for everyone" (Keeley and Morlock, 1988, p. 3).

A second model for delivering access to credit is used frequently in Third World countries, including several Latin American countries, India, African nations, and Bangladesh. This model makes use of "peer groups" — small (four to six members) groups of people who are each pursuing a business activity and are well-acquainted with each other. The group chooses two of its members to receive the first loans; additional members receive loans only after a pattern of repayment of these initial loans has been firmly established. Continued access to credit is contingent on the clear credit record of the group as a whole.

In Canada, the Calmeadow Foundation has assisted Native Canadian women living on three reserves who are operating businesses in the informal economy and need cash to purchase equipment or supplies. On two of these reserves, banks do not accept collateral from Native people, because their homes and land are owned by the Tribe. On the third reserve, there is no bank to serve Native people at all. Under Calmeadow's programme, small loans are made by the Toronto Dominion Bank (and guaranteed by the Calmeadow Foundation) initially to two women in organised peer groups. When the two women have paid back their loans, two more women can borrow.

In Chicago, Illinois, the Women's Self-Employment Project (WSEP), an organisation targeted primarily to low-income, Black women, has initiated a micro loan fund making use of the peer group process. First-time borrowers are limited to $1 500 and required to open a savings account from which withdrawals can be made only after six months. Peer group members meet bi-weekly for one hour to make loan payments. They also act as support for one another and receive technical assistance from Project staff.

A similar model operates in France through the intermediary Fondation Femin'Autres. Femin'Autres forms small groups of women who then save and lend money to group members with viable business ideas. These groups are called "Tontines" after the solidarity groups of women in French-speaking Africa. "Ten women decide to save FF 500 each month to contribute to the new business of one of them. After four months another FF 20 000 will be saved and one of them can start up. Another woman takes her place, and after four months she too can invest the FF 20 000 in her new business. This procedure could be repeated again, after which three businesses would have been created and nine women each save FF 6 000, reimbursed with interest" (Femin'Autres, 1986).

All three of these programmes, as well as the Third World models on which they are based, are relatively new and their results are being followed with interest.

Finally, other intermediaries provide access to credit by establishing relationships with conventional lenders. One mechanism that involves a conventional lender is a loan guarantee programme. Women's World Banking (WWB), an international women's organisation promoting access to credit, utilises this model as one of its programme options. WWB has affiliates in over 33 countries around the world. While the majority of affiliates operate in Third World countries, the appeal of this mechanism is growing among intermediaries in "developed" countries.

Under the WWB loan guarantee programme, which is one of five programmes available to affiliates, access to credit is facilitated in the following way. Local women organise a WWB affiliate or an already existing women's organisation affiliates with the WWB network and raises an initial capital fund. That amount is matched two-to-one by the international WWB fund. The total pool of money is then available as a guarantee against 75 per cent of the amount of any loan made by a participating local bank to an eligible woman.

WWB has eight affiliates in OECD countries: three in France, three in the U.S., one each in the Netherlands, Italy, Spain and Canada. Two new affiliate programmes are in formation in the U.S. and new programmes are forming in Canada, Sweden, Switzerland, England, Spain and New Zealand. Only the West Virginia affiliate currently operates a loan guarantee fund, but Femin'Autres, which is a WWB affiliate in France, and the U.S. affiliate in Philadelphia are working to establish a fund.

Not all WWB affiliates, however, utilise this programme mechanism to provide access to credit. ADIEF, one of the three WWB French affiliates, has recently focused on the creation of a financing tool for disadvantaged women and on promoting an information exchange among business women. ADIEF is also participating in a business advisory programme through the "Maison d'Information des Femmes," a governmental agency. Through this programme, ADIEF reviews business plans of women business owners and provides referral information.

The WWB loan guarantee mechanism frequently leads to compromise on the part of both intermediaries and participating banks. While the affiliate's social goal is to increase women's access to credit, all loan applicants under the loan guarantee programme must be acceptable to the bank concerned. Operating in this context, a WWB affiliate often becomes more conservative in considering whether to guarantee a loan, and the bank's behaviour often becomes less risk averse. Over time, an educational process takes place that is beneficial to both the affiliate and the bank.

In Australia, the Victoria Women's Trust combines a women's foundation that targets women's economic development organisations with a Guaranteed Loan Fund (GLF). Originally funded by the Victorian government, the Trust initiated the GLF because:

"Lack of personal savings and/or traditional forms of collateral, isolation, lack of self-confidence, lack of credibility in the economic arena, lack of access to credit are all factors which deter low-income women from choosing self-employment" (Victoria Women's Trust, 1987, p. 4).

FGIF

The Fonds de Garantie pour la Création, la Reprise ou le Développement d'Entreprise à l'Initiative des Femmes (FGIF) is a new loan guarantee fund in France designed to assist in the start-up, buy-out, and development of women-owned businesses. It was implemented in January 1989 by an official agreement between the French public authorities and the Institute for the Development of the Social Economy (IDES). Operational since May 1989, the fund has already assisted over a hundred women entrepreneurs.

The fund guarantees start-up investment for a business and also covers the needs of a revolving loan fund that lends to new and small businesses (creation or buy-out) no more than five years old. Businesses can apply for these two types of assistance, which guarantee loans up to a maximum of FF 50 000 each, simultaneously. Applications are accepted and reviewed by a regional delegation or the local representatives for Women's Rights who gave technical assistance, information and advice to the business owner. If the applicant's chosen bank allocates credit conditional on a guarantee, the bank then works through IDES, which monitors the loan docket. Loan guarantee decisions are made by a committee with national stature, chaired by a representative of the Secretary of State for Women's Rights.

Under the terms of a guarantee contract negotiated with the State Bank Victoria, the Trust guarantees 50 per cent of certain loans made to women by the Bank. The remaining 50 per cent is guaranteed by the Fund. Eligible businesses must be unable to access credit from traditional sources, employ 50 per cent women, have 25 per cent owner's equity, and follow a "responsible industrial policy including the payment of award wages to employees and the observance of equal opportunity and affirmative action principles" (Victoria Women's Trust, 1987).

WEDCO has pursued another type of strategy involving a unique relationship with a conventional lender. Early in its development, WEDCO approached the First Bank System in Minneapolis/St. Paul with an arrangement through which the bank would increase its lending activity to certain women-owned businesses. Under the arrangement, the bank has assigned loan officers from within its consumer lending division to work with WEDCO staff and clients. Clients approach the bank with well-prepared loan proposals, and bank loan officers actively negotiate the collateral and equity requirements of each loan. This working relationship has resulted in loans ranging from $1 000 to $60 000 to many businesses that previously would have been denied conventional financing.

Low-cost Space

Some intermediary organisations and programmes offer space in which very small, new businesses pay below market rents and share the cost of a range of services with other new businesses. The Markthalle in Frankfurt, for example, provides space and day care services for women-owned businesses, as well as temporary personnel on an emergency basis when family responsibilities require women to leave their shops. The need for the Markthalle was identified during women-only training courses offered by its sister programme, Frauenbetriebe, which trains unemployed women to become independent entrepreneurs. The Markthalle is run as a co-operative; the site is collectively equipped and managed and funds are pooled from the co-operative members to assist women opening new shops. The Markthalle is subsidised by the Ministry of Labour in Bonn, as well as by other government agencies, including the city of Frankfurt, which shares in the cost of management consultants.

Strengthening Personal Effectiveness and Meeting Personal Needs

Many women who decide to investigate self-employment and small business development opportunities face barriers related to their personal circumstances. Some women, for example, lose the support of their family and friends when they decide to start a business, while others have child or dependent care responsibilities that they must meet in the context of business ownership. To assist women in these areas, many intermediary programmes have developed methods, often built into training curricula, to affirm women's self-confidence, build their skills in assessing and making wise use of available resources, and assist them in identifying and meeting their personal and family needs.

For example, at the Women's Economic Development Corporation:

"We begin our Self-Employment Training Programme with four days of Personal Effectiveness. These courses allow the women to look at their goals, their behavior, their backgrounds, their support systems and evaluate what they want to keep and what they want to change for the future.... They also need to build up some reserve of energy because being a small business owner is isolating and full of problems that need immediate attention. Building this reserve of energy through a new support system is very important in creating opportunities for future business activities" (Keeley and Morlock, 1988, p. 2).

Similarly, in the screening or pre-assessment phase of the training at the Women's Self-Employment Project, clients are asked questions concerning their child care arrangements, their family history with regard to such problems as spouse abuse or alcoholism, and their credit history. Often, the answers to these questions reveal areas that must be addressed before a woman pursues self-employment.

Special Programmes for Women Receiving Public Assistance

Women who receive benefits from public assistance programmes (called "welfare" in the U.S. and social security in England and Canada) face particular barriers in the process of becoming self-employed. Many of these barriers are created by the policies and regulations that govern programme implementation. For example, in the United States, a woman's welfare benefits will cease if she acquires business assets in excess of $1 000, and she immediately loses Medicaid benefits for both herself and her children when she leaves the welfare rolls.

In several Western European countries, and to a lesser extent in Canada, programmes have been developed to encourage the self-employment efforts of people on public assistance. The Chômeurs-Créateurs programme in France and the Enterprise Allowance scheme in Britain, for example, allow men and women who are unemployed and/or receiving public assistance to continue to receive their benefits for a period of time while they attempt business start-up. Women's participation in these programmes is relatively low: in 1982, almost 19 per cent of French participants were women; the comparable figure in Britain was approximately 22 per cent (Bendick and Egan, 1986).

The French authorities have recently introduced measures to give greater financial support to women, particularly if they have stopped working for personal reasons or been unemployed.

In Canada, the Community Futures programme operates a Self-Employment Incentive Option in targeted areas of high unemployment. Under the programme, unemployed people pursuing self-employment are eligible to receive 52 weeks of public assistance benefits. Approximately 34 per cent of participants in this programme are women.

High Visibility Public Policy and Advocacy Efforts

A small number of intermediaries concentrate their efforts on advocacy to create a supportive public policy environment that enables women to realise their self-employment dreams. By analysing the barriers that women face to business start-up or expansion and designing appropriate remedies, such organisations use their skills in the policy arena to achieve structural change in the conditions that impede women's progress. A participant from the United States at the Oslo Conference (May 1987) termed it "going one step further":

"We think that we need better business plans, more markets, more classes on taxes and employee benefits to be successful. It is true that the more knowledge a business owner has, the better off he or she is going to be. However, there are real barriers to success for female entrepreneurs. Until the organisations that we create, or that exist to help us, recognise that advocacy by and for us is part of the answer to our need, we will have to struggle along on our own. Organisations must go a step beyond providing information and education and be advocates for women business owners" (Weiss, 1987, p. 5).

In each of the OECD countries, public policy does, whether intentionally or unintentionally, present unique barriers to women attempting business start-up. In Sweden, for example, a new subsidy designed to benefit unemployed people starting a business placed its highest priority on manufacturing firms, an industry sector in which relatively few women participate. In the Netherlands, a programme assisting new start-ups requires a 10 per cent cash match, a difficult requirement for low-income women to meet. In Portugal, excessive paperwork and red tape required of rural women means that few can take advantage of government credit programmes aimed at business start-ups. And in the U.S., women receiving assistance through the Federal Aid to Families with Dependent Children (AFDC) programme are not allowed to separate their business and personal assets when attempting business start-up.

In the last few years, a growing number of organisations in the United States have attempted to remove the barriers faced by women who choose the option of self-employment as a way to move away from public assistance. In West Virginia, for example, the legislature passed a bill authorising a pilot entrepreneurship project for a small group of women on welfare. The bill requires the W.V. Department of Human Services to implement the project by applying to the federal government for a waiver of restrictive AFDC regulations. Success in this effort was due in large part to the advocacy work of Women and Employment, an intermediary whose clients include women receiving welfare benefits.

The Corporation for Enterprise Development (CfED) in Washington, D.C. is building on this experience and that of two other states, Illinois and Minnesota, who have substituted state monies for federal public assistance funds as a way to get around restrictive federal barriers. CfED is sponsoring a multi-year demonstration project under which five states have obtained waivers from the federal government to pilot self-employment training and support programmes for AFDC participants in selected locations.

Examples of broad-based advocacy efforts are found in other OECD countries as well. In Portugal, according to Ana Maria Braga Da Cruz, the Comissão da Condicão Feminina in Porto clearly sees its role as responding to the voices of the rural women it serves in Northern Portugal. "We know that it is not the experts team who will transform the 'milieu'. Local people have the big role. The experts give support, giving answers, always reformulating and adapting." In England, the Women's Enterprise Development Agency (WEDA) developed a series of seminars that brought bankers and women in business together to talk about the barriers women faced in seeking capital. Women pointed out, for example, that while a father of three children is considered to be stable and reliable, a mother with three children to look after is regarded as unstable and unreliable. WEDA reports at least one concrete achievement from these efforts — a highly visible service offering advice to women in business. The service will be available in city centres and staffed by women bankers.

DEVELOPING NEW INTERMEDIARY ORGANISATIONS AND PROGRAMMES

How are new intermediary organisations and programmes initiated? While the answer varies from country to country and locality to locality, some form of needs assessment is often the first step. Community needs assessment involves naming and understanding the barriers faced by women and mobilising resources in the community to overcome them. The needs assessment process often brings together public and private organisations to work in partnership toward common goals.

The authors of the *Working Guide to Women's Self-Employment* identify four tasks in a needs assessment process:

— Gauge the interest in enterprise development among local women of all income levels and all racial and ethnic backgrounds;
— Explore, with local women, their experience with business ownership, and identify the particular barriers they face and opportunities they see in the process of business start-up and expansion;
— Learn about the support services (i.e. training and technical assistance, sources of financing, and day care) available for local micro-enterprises and small businesses;
— Communicate the information gained to key individuals in the community, and enlist the investment of their resources and expertise in responsive new and expanded strategies (Gould and Lyman, 1987, p.83).

Two examples from widely different locations demonstrate how a needs assessment process can lay the groundwork for intermediary programme development. In Haarlem, the Netherlands, the Chamber of Commerce was persuaded by its first female Board member, Lia Kroskinski, to take seriously a report prepared by Haarlem women's organisations that accused the Chamber of being "women unfriendly". As a result, Kroskinski was appointed to chair a committee to investigate: 1) how women's entrepreneurship could be encouraged and 2) how the Chamber could be of assistance. The committee's work began with an inventory of area business resources and advisory committees and of bottlenecks faced by women. The committee decided to host a symposium to which everyone in the community would be invited. Six hundred people attended and identified additional barriers faced by women to business ownership. They stressed the need to educate young women in secondary schools about business ownership and to show them examples of successful women in their own community who had pursued this option.

Chamber officials were immediately persuaded to hire a woman to advise other women. This represented a stunning turn around — before the symposium Chamber officials had said, "Information for starters is information for starters; whether they are women or men, it makes no difference" (OECD, 1987a). Faced with an audience of 600 people, however, they quickly changed their opinion. The newly appointed women's business adviser provides business advice to women two days each week. The Chamber has also initiated a mentor programme and made recommendations regarding the length of entrepreneurial training in the vocational school.

A second example of a needs assessment undertaken in Western Australia took its shape from a U.S. organisation, the National Coalition for Women's Enterprise (formerly known as Hub Co-ventures). The Hub community-based needs assessment process has several key steps:

— Assessing the community for those individuals and institutions already sensitive to the potential for women's business ownership and involving them directly in the process;
— Identifying women business owners (WBOs) and women with an active interest in self-employment (WWIs);
— Collecting data on local women business owners and on the types, location, profitability, level of employment, and start-up capitalisation of their businesses;
— Bringing WBOs and WWIs together to network and to identify barriers and opportunities for business development;
— Documenting existing training/technical assistance, financing and day care services;
— Formulating and presenting initial recommendations to community leaders for new or restructured local services (Gould and Lyman, 1987, p. 86).

Following a visit from HUB's founder and president Jing Lyman, the Western Australian Department of Employment and Training, Women's Economic Development Office, commenced a year-long study of women's enterprise development. In July 1988, the Department issued the Hub Report, which recommends:

1. Establishing a comprehensive data base on female entrepreneurs in Western Australia;
2. Compiling a resource handbook for women;
3. Establishing a women's enterprise centre that would administer a revolving loan fund;
4. Increasing the resources available to women's small business development courses;
5. Increasing access to resources for aboriginal, migrant and rural women; and
6. Requesting the state government to work with the federal government to establish a tax deduction for child care expenses.

According to the Department's director, "While the personal and social implications of the HUB Project cannot be overlooked, neither can we underestimate the significant income-generating potential which women in business represent to our economy" (Western Australian Department of Employment and Training, 1988, p. 1). In this case, a community needs assessment process sparked new programme directions and has motivated Australia's Eastern Region Economic and Employment Committee to launch a similar project.

Funding for Intermediary Programmes

Intermediaries promoting women's local employment initiatives face a barrier shared by many other women's organisations: how can they adequately fund activities that serve women, a constituency that has not attracted its share of available resources and can often afford only minimal fees for services received? The implications of this question are clearly stated by the West German author of a paper delivered at the OECD conference in Oslo:

> "Clearly, the target group for these projects, unemployed women, are totally incapable of financing such endeavours themselves. Thus, the financial situation of the women's work projects is highly differentiated, ranging from those groups not (yet) receiving any support to those completely in the black, including the means to finance paid administrators. In the Federal Republic we have several general and progressive government agencies administering public funds. However, not one of the supporting women's work projects has long-term financial security. As a result, not only are the women employed by such projects themselves in danger of being made redundant, but also the expertise accrued in areas of education and consultancy for women's work projects may well be lost" (Haas, 1987, p. 7).

In OECD countries, funding for new organisations and expanded programmes related to women's business ownership has come from both the public and private sectors. The proportion of support coming from each sector, however, varies considerably by country. In the European countries, Canada and Australia, public funds from local, state and national authorities have played the major role in supporting needs assessment efforts and new programme initiatives. Examples in Denmark and the Netherlands have already been cited. In Canada, the Community Futures programme, sponsored by the federal government to support initiatives in economically distressed communities, supports training programmes attended by large numbers of women. In each of these countries, the private philanthropic sector is relatively small.

The situation is quite different in the United States. While most states and many localities offer assistance to women attempting to procure government contracts, less than 1 per cent of women-owned businesses actually obtain contracts (Committee on Small Business, 1988, p. 19). The level of resources available from the federal government reached its peak during the Carter Administration and has dwindled steadily since. The recently enacted "Women's Business Ownership Act of 1988" provides for "financial assistance to private organisations to conduct demonstration projects for the benefit of small business concerns owned and controlled by women". The relatively low appropriation level, however, allowed for the funding of only four demonstration projects.

On the other hand, the private philanthropic sector is very strong in the United States. A growing number of private philanthropic organisations, including private foundations, corporations and religious institutions, provide support to local women's business development efforts, particularly if they target low-income women and minority women to receive their services. WEDCO and Women and Employment, for example, currently depend on private foundations and corporations for approximately 70 per cent of their annual operating budgets.

The problem of sustained support for women's enterprise development programmes remains. As new interests and priorities emerge to compete for currently available funds, how will women's enterprise initiatives hold the interest of funders and build a diversified and stable base of support? At least two strategies hold some promise. Organisations can become entrepreneurial themselves and engage in projects to generate income for their own support, such as real estate ventures or other business-related activity. Organisations can also build a base of financial and political support among their clients. A well-organised constituency plays a key role in keeping the women's enterprise development agenda high on the priority list of local, state and national governments. International organisations such as the Soroptomists and the Business and Professional Women's Clubs already play this role. Building this kind of support is a long-term strategy and requires careful planning; in the long run, however, it may be the most effective way to focus both public and private sector attention on women entrepreneurs and their vital role in the economic development of their communities.

CONCLUSION

This chapter has reviewed the role that intermediary organisations and programmes in the OECD countries play currently in strengthening women's self-employment activities. A wide variety of intermediaries now provide innovative training, credit programmes and a range of other services to a growing number of women pursuing self-employment. As these organisations and programmes develop and mature, and as new ones start-up, they are becoming ever more effective advocates for women. This process is crucial, for it is only when women's concerns reach the policy arena that the long-term, systemic changes necessary to ensure women's place in economic development can be realised.

A key step in this process is the exchange of information among intermediaries in different countries. In this regard, the Women's Bureau of the Commission of the European Communities has taken a lead role. In October 1987 at a conference co-sponsored by the Commission, CEDEFOP and the French Délégation à la Condition Féminine, Odile Quintin, head of the Women's Bureau, named two areas for immediate action: 1) the exchange of information between practitioners, including the development of network structures to benefit women and self-employment activities internationally, and 2) political and legislative initiatives (European Centre for the Development of Vocational Training, 1987). Prior to this conference, the EEC commissioned a major research project on "Business Creation by Women: Motivations, Situations and Perspectives". Using information from this study and the results of the Conference, the Women's Bureau initiated a series of explorations into the networks that exist in the 12 EEC countries among women's local employment initiatives and the intermediaries that support them. In the final report from France, the authors described how the simple act of searching for intermediaries began to create the network and elicit information not available previously (Halpern and Rerolle, 1988, p. 1).

The EEC is clearly carrying out its resolve to provide for an exchange of information. Regarding legislative reform, its first target is an examination of women's lack of access to credit. Unfortunately there is no counterpart in North America to this kind of national or international networking.

The activity generated by the OECD and the EEC has indeed focused attention on women entrepreneurs. As a result of their efforts, mainstream economic developers are taking notice. Only time will tell if all this activity at the local, national and international level meets the needs of Shirley, Josefa, Jane and Marie-Claire that were described at the beginning of this chapter. The actions of these women and their counterparts will make a great difference in local, regional and national economies. The Director of the Women's Commission in Porto, Portugal, stated it this way:

"We believe that equal opportunities and the increase of women's social participation can be achieved only through better information and better support to women and women's groups.

Women need places of information and thought which enable them to decide about their future, to intervene in the decisions of their country, their family and their lives. The groups we work with taught us that, when informed and motivated, women have a kind of intervention which provides innovative alternatives concerning areas which worry everyone: development, employment, family life and education".

It is up to all OECD countries, the current intermediaries and policy makers to provide such a place.

REFERENCES

Bendick, Marc and Mary Lou Egan (1986) "Transfer Payment Diversion for Self-Employment Initiatives: British and French Experience", Paper presented at the Conference on Self-employment, Racine, Wisconsin, 16-18 July.

Bottrup, Pernille (1988) "Det er friheden der traekker...: Evaluering af et Ivaerksaetterkursus for Evinder i Storstoms", Amt. Teknologisk Institute, Taastrup, Denmark.

Committee on Small Business (1988) "New Economic Realities: The Rise of Women Entrepreneurs", Report 100-736, House of Representatives, Washington, D.C., June.

European Centre for the Development of Vocational Training (1987) "Women and the Creation of Enterprises: Summary Report on the Conference in Sophia Antipolis" (France), 21-23 October.

Fémin'Autres, Brochure, 1986.

Gould, Sara K. and Jing Lyman (1987) *A Working Guide to Women's Self-Employment*, Corporation for Enterprise Development, Washington, D.C.

Haas, Lu (1987) "Frauenbetriebe: Support and Training for Women's Local Employment Initiatives", OECD, Paris, May.

Halpern, Monique and Marie-France Rerolle (1988) "Report on the Activities of the European Support Network to Women's ILE in France", Institut de la Coopération Sociale Internationale and Retravailler Rhône-Alpes, July.

Keeley, Kathryn and Jan Morlock (1988) "Results of Targeting Self-Employment Programmes to Low Income Women", unpublished paper prepared for Tufts University, Boston, Mass., March.

OECD (1987a) "Presentation of Lia Kroskinski-de Keulenaar" OECD, (1987b).

OECD (1987b) "Seminar Record of Second International Seminar on Women — Local Initiatives — Job Creation", Paris.

Storstroms County LMO (Labour Market Office) (1987) "Storstroms County Entrepreneur Project", May.

Van der Meer, Leni (1986) "A Survey of Women Entrepreneurs and Support Organisations in the Netherlands", European Centre for the Development of Vocational Training, Rotterdam, September.

Victoria Women's Trust (1987) "Second Annual Report, 1986-87", internal document.

Weiss, Chris (1987) "Going One Step Further: An Advocacy Approach to Women and Entrepreneurial Development", OECD, Paris, May.

Western Australian Department of Employment and Training (1988) "The Hub Project News", June.

Wickmann, Jane and Elizabeth Sundin (1987) "Women's Businesses in Denmark and Sweden and Other Nordic Countries", OECD, Paris, May.

Women's Enterprise Development Agency (1986) "A Proposal to Establish the First Women's Enterprise Development Agency in the United Kingdom", internal document.

Chapter V

THE ROLE OF INTERMEDIARIES
IN STRENGTHENING WOMEN'S BUSINESS EXPANSION ACTIVITIES

Kathryn Keeley

INTRODUCTION

Although intermediaries that assist women to become self-employed attract most public attention, these agencies can also assist self-employed women to expand their businesses. Many women in the OECD countries already own firms, but the vast majority are very small in terms of employment and receipts. This chapter focuses on the role of intermediaries in strengthening the expansion of women's business activities.

The expansion of women-owned businesses is a topic needing further analysis and research. Little information currently exists on the growth of women's businesses in OECD countries. There is little research on the successes or problems of expanding women-owned companies. The interest in assisting women to expand their businesses is very new, and the issues in this area are just emerging. Therefore, this chapter concentrates on what needs to be accomplished, rather than what has already happened.

THE IMPORTANCE OF BUSINESS EXPANSION

Business expansion can be defined as "moving beyond self-employment" by adding one or more permanent full-time employees. This definition of business expansion appropriately focuses attention on the complexities associated with growth, such as managing people, formalising operations, and taking greater risk. Expansion can also be defined as it relates to growth in sales: women who hope to expand their enterprises have higher sales goals than do most self-employed women. This definition highlights other complexities associated with growth, such as the need for a broader vision of the firm, a greater commitment of time by the owner, and more strategic thinking.

Business expansion is not an appropriate goal for all self-employed women or men. Some people are content to run very small ventures. They already meet their own needs and do not want to commit more time to, or change the nature of, their businesses. The firms may be successful, yet do not necessarily have growth potential. Some businesses serve a small market where there is little room for growth. Others provide a service which only they can provide, and they are already meeting all the demand they can serve on their own. Many successful self-employed women would be unsuccessful managers in the more complex environment of a larger enterprise.

At the same time, there are several reasons why it is important for women, who have the interest and ability to do so, to be able to move beyond self-employment. First, women bring new talent, product and service ideas, and management approaches to a world economy seeking economic growth and innovation. Their economic contribution could be an important resource for all OECD countries in a time of rapid industrial change. Women who own businesses in growing sectors can build companies, create jobs and contribute new wealth to their communities.

Second, for women to become significant players in the world economy, they must create jobs, manage large corporations, and become partners in shaping economic policy in their countries. Women will be better able to challenge the *status quo* in economic development and redirect resources towards women when they manage large organisations and accumulate wealth of their own. Large business owners command respect. These individuals have the ability to influence economic and social policy, such as child care and health care, which have a great effect on women's lives. Women business owners could be influential in redirecting national resources to benefit other women. They could also use their wealth to invest in the business opportunities of other women. As more women own and run large enterprises, all women will gain respect in the business community. Without the respect of the traditional business community, women will remain marginalised and their businesses will be stuck in a "pink-collar ghetto".

Finally, an important benefit of women expanding their businesses is that they create new role models. Women who operate successful small businesses will be role models for others. They will help remove the barriers women currently face in almost every economy in the world.

BARRIERS TO EXPANSION

Women face both personal barriers and external barriers to expanding their businesses. These barriers are often familiar to women business owners. They had to overcome them to start up their businesses. The familiarity of these barriers makes it no less difficult for women when they reappear in new forms with different ramifications.

Personal Barriers

Self-employed women may face several personal barriers as they begin planning to expand their businesses or to run larger enterprises. The first barrier is women's responsibility for children and their personal commitment to family. Women still bear primary responsibility for child care and dependent family members. Self-employed women frequently express concern about the conflict between increased responsibility for an expanded business and the need to manage their personal and family lives (WEDCO, Business Clinic, 1988). Often family responsibility is what forced women to leave other employment and seek the flexibility of self-employment in the first place (Stevenson, 1986). Self-employment allowed them to control their own time, to set their own goals and to structure a business that fits their family responsibilities. From a woman's viewpoint, an expanded business could jeopardise this independence and control of time. Many women refuse to explore the idea of expansion because of the need to balance work commitment with time at home.

The second personal barrier for women is an aversion to risk in the business environment. Joan Sweeney, in her research on the Committee of 200, a U.S. network of women who own and/or run large enterprises, found that women have different perspectives on risk-taking than men. According to Sweeney, people feel most comfortable in their ability to accept risk if they firmly believe they can recoup their losses. Even self-employed women frequently do not believe they can recoup financial loss. Any loss is viewed as permanent (Walker, 1988). This perspective on risk blocks many women, even those women who have chosen to start businesses, from having the confidence to expand their businesses. They view expansion less as an opportunity than as an unnecessary risk.

Women's third personal barrier is not having a broad vision for their company. Research indicates that women who succeed often believe their success is due to luck rather than planning. This attitude prohibits women from having a larger vision for their career generally and, more specifically, for their businesses. Women are generally socialised into thinking of themselves in helping roles rather than as the chief executives of large enterprises (Nelton, 1987). Women are reluctant to think big and dream out loud about their ideas. Women's personal support systems can be negative and limit their ability to develop a vision for their companies. Women also have few female role models who have a broad horizon for their companies. The ability to maintain an ever-expanding business vision is an atypical skill for many women (Therrien, 1986).

The fourth barrier women face is the lack of personal experience with business expansions. Women have had few opportunities to establish new product lines or divisions as employees of a corporation. These risk-taking opportunities are most often given to men. Many male entrepreneurs have this experience before leaving corporations to start their own businesses. This hands-on experience of growing a business provides an important set of skills and a personal confidence level that even sucessfully self-employed women have not had the opportunity to develop.

Finally, many women lack the management experience necessary to run a larger enterprise. They have not already served as managers in large corporations. Once an employee is hired, the role of the owner changes to supervisor, with the accompanying need to delegate, share information, hire and fire. Entrepreneurial literature describes the transition of an entrepreneur to a manager as a difficult phase for most business owners. This transition can be particularly difficult for women who have not had prior management experience. The role of manager continually changes as a company expands and more employees are hired. A manager must have the ability to be a leader and instil a vision of the company in all her employees. She moves from doing to inspiring, setting policy, leading and facilitating. Women find these roles difficult. They must often leave behind a "friendship" style in order to maintain boundaries between themselves and their employees.

External Barriers

Women also may face external barriers to business expansion. The first barrier is the general perception of women business owners described in chapter III. Self-employed women are perceived as having hobbies, as opposed to being serious-minded business people capable of, and interested in, expanding their companies; in particular, women who have children are stereotyped as having family concerns which come first (Nelton, 1987). For some women this is true, but others have the ability to balance having families and expanding their businesses.

The fact that a majority of women-owned businesses are in the service sector compounds the negative perception of these businesses. Service sector businesses are often viewed as offering few financial rewards for a community, let alone the economy of a country. While this image is beginning to change, it still functions as a barrier for most women.

A second external barrier which inhibits the expansion of women's businesses is lack of capital, and, in particular, inability to finance increased cash-flow needs through each phase of expansion. The working capital needs of a growing company — to finance marketing, inventory, increased personnel and other overheads — may be greater than current income can provide. Women need equity capital, or very patient debt, to finance expansions.

Women who already own small businesses seem to face the same obstacles in raising capital as women just starting out. Even though they have established a track record, they still cannot attract investments from the typical sources. Equity, for example, is typically raised through private offerings of stock to family, friends, acquaintances or business associates. Unfortunately, few families are willing to invest in their female relatives (Goffee and Scase, 1987, p. 11). Few women have the resources to provide capital to other women business-owners. Women are not part of the existing "angel networks", as they are called in the United States. Venture capital in the U.S. and the growing venture capital markets in the EEC countries are, for the most part, dominated and controlled by men. Women have limited access to these men and, as a result, to equity capital. Expanding businesses can use debt to finance equipment, real estate and, in some cases, working capital. However, debt is difficult for women to obtain for many of the same reasons that equity is scarce. In addition, since a majority of women-owned businesses are in the service sector, the obstacles to raising expansion capital through debt are compounded (Therrien, 1986). Without hard assets that can be committed as collateral, financing is not available.

At the same time, women lack the personal assets which can be invested in their business or pledged for expansion loans. Their businesses are still too small to have allowed them to accumulate a large net worth. And, as when women start a business, they are frequently unable to invest family assets in their businesses. Even their personal wealth is often viewed as family wealth and the ability for a female family member to risk it in a business can be limited. Their financial status not only traps women in enterprises which need little capital, but also limits their potential to expand their enterprises (Therrien, 1986).

APPROPRIATE SERVICES
FOR INTERMEDIARIES HELPING EXPANDING BUSINESSES

The techniques of intermediaries assisting women who want to start businesses must change when they begin to work with expanding businesses. Some of the services required — such as personal support, development of confidence and new skills, access to capital and provision of role models — are similar to those needed by women pursuing self-employment. However, there are new service requirements and differences in emphasis in the areas of management, finance and business structure for an intermediary working with expanding businesses.

Management

Management can be very difficult for women who do not have prior business experience. Intermediaries can assist women in acquiring the necessary skills. In workshops conducted by WEDCO in the United States, women often report that their businesses are run like a family, with everyone involved in everything (WEDCO, 1988). Women need assistance in clarifying job descriptions and lines of authority. They need suggestions on how to delegate responsibility. They need expert advice on establishing personnel policies which meet their value systems, setting boundaries for acceptable performance, and allowing for growth and change in the company (Nelton, 1986). Programmes such as those developed in the U.K., France and Germany offer appropriate skill-building workshops for women business owners.

Intermediaries may be called upon as consultants to women business owners to point out when additions to the workforce will require management changes and what personnel challenges and crises are likely to occur as the company grows. Intermediaries can ensure that conflicts are accepted as a normal part of the growth process rather than as personal inadequacy on the part of the business owner. New boundaries are being forged in the company, and the intermediary can provide a support system as the changes occur. Business owners also need accurate information about legal and labour issues in order to implement new management systems.

Finance

From WEDCO's work in the field and conversations with intermediaries in the U.K., France, Spain and Canada, it is apparent that women identify raising capital as the greatest obstacle to expanding their businesses. The U.S.-based National Association of Women Business Owners (NAWBO) continually raises access to capital as a major issue in all of its public testimony and hearings. There has been much discussion of solutions to this problem, yet few new models have been developed.

Intermediaries could develop programmes to assist women in broadening their contacts or networks when seeking financing. They could develop their own list of "angels" who are willing to invest in women's companies. They could play a role in screening and advising businesses on behalf of investors. Introductions to, and contacts with, borrowers would be facilitated through the intermediary. In addition, intermediaries could develop investment funds which they manage and control, to forge a path for other investors. Examples of some of these approaches were provided in chapter IV. For example, the French organisation Femin' Autres brings together groups of women who jointly invest their savings in order to make loans to members of the group (OECD, 1987).

Business Structure

The business owner who is expanding and adding employees will need consulting assistance in making structural changes in her business. Tax filing and government licence requirements may be different. In some cases, a change in legal form — as from sole proprietorship to corporation — will facilitate growth. More sophisticated capital-raising plans may require more formal business controls. Legal and management advice is needed to make optimal structural choices.

THE DESIGN OF INTERMEDIARIES

Service delivery mechanisms, overall programme structure, financial services, staff expertise and funding sources may not be the same for programmes serving women who want to expand their existing businesses as for self-employment programmes. Existing intermediaries will need toadd new programmes. New intermediaries must decide whether to serve only expanding businesses, or both new and expanding businesses.

If an intermediary decides to address the needs of expanding businesses, its goals for women who participate in training programmes or receive consulting advice will be unlike those for self-employment programmes. Programme goals should focus on job creation and increased productivity, rather than increases in family income or personal self-confidence. At the same time, and as with self-employment programmes, success must be judged by whether women achieve goals which may be unique to each of their businesses.

In addition, intermediaries confront a different type and level of risk in working with expanding businesses. Expansion involves a significant risk of failure for businesses that are currently solvent. Intermediaries need to incorporate this risk into their programme goals. They should take into account projected failure rates and business closings when they determine how they will measure their success.

Women who are expanding their businesses require different delivery mechanisms. While self-employment programmes tend to use training programmes and short-term contacts with the client, programmes which serve expanding businesses must offer more long-term and personalised consulting. Client contact is often more intense than in self-employment programmes. Intermediaries may need to concentrate their resources and limit themselves to helping a very small number of businesses each year.

Programme Structure

There are three general approaches which intermediaries can adopt to serve women who want to expand their businesses. Which of these three approaches makes the most sense depends entirely on local needs and preferences.

First, it is possible for intermediaries to develop programmes to work with individuals who seek self-employment, and then assist those clients who choose to expand, on a case-by-case basis. However, at some point this approach becomes frustrating for the intermediary and the client. The client's needs will outstrip the ability of the intermediary. The staff will not be prepared to meet the needs of an expanding business. Business owners will be left to find other resources or go it alone and rely on the intermediary for support when they are in crisis.

A second, and probably more effective, approach is for an intermediary deliberately to establish a programme for growing businesses, with its own goals, objectives and services. Then, the intermediary can plan specific training programmes and actively encourage expansion activity among its clients. One challenge for the intermediary which decides to serve both types of businesses is that it may already be stereotyped as a self-employment organisation. Women business owners may not want to be identified with a women's agency which has a reputation built on self-employment for a specific client population. They may perceive association with the intermediary as putting them at a disadvantage in pursuing financing or business consulting. The intermediary will need to take steps to expand its image to appeal to already successful business women.

A third approach is for the intermediary to focus exclusively on expanding businesses, which may mean helping a much smaller clientele. Their resources are concentrated on fewer individuals, especially if they are financing the businesses. A dedicated intermediary may have a better image among business women. However, it will have fewer contacts with women business owners who might really need its assistance. An intermediary which only serves expanding businesses also requires a much larger base of existing business women who might become clients to justify its formation.

Structure of Financial Services

Intermediaries which serve expanding businesses will be called upon to assist clients with financing. Financing can either be offered by the intermediary or the intermediary can refer clients elsewhere. Before an intermediary makes this decision, it must determine whether it has, or can acquire, the skills and resources to make the required investments. Investing in expanding businesses can require much greater knowledge of finance than providing small seed loans to women seeking self-employment. With long-term debt, the goal is repayment of the loan. With equity, it is enhanced value of the firm. Judging either requires expertise. An intermediary should also determine whether it will be more successful in attracting capital to women's businesses by creating its own capital pool or developing contacts with existing sources of capital.

Staff

Staff must provide competent management consulting and sometimes very sophisticated financial advice to their clients. Before doing so, they must either cultivate in-house expertise or develop relationships with lawyers, tax experts and business consultants. Since most intermediaries hire generalists who can work with a variety of businesses, they will have to develop a network of individuals with expertise in specific industries.

By developing their own networks, intermediaries play an important role in increasing the ability of women's businesses to make contacts which can lead to sales and information-sharing. Corporate volunteers in management, financing and marketing can be an important resource. In some countries, large corporations are willing to release staff on secondment or loan executives, who provide specific consulting to a variety of businesses.

Staff expertise is especially important if an intermediary decides to offer financing to its clients. Both long-term debt and equity investing require an understanding of business owners' cash flow, assets, credit history and sales potential. Equity investing requires, in addition, an understanding of the individual's management capabilities and their vision for the company. Staff must have these skills and know how to structure debt and equity arrangements.

Fundraising

Economic development resources to work with expanding businesses are limited. Intermediaries which choose to serve expanding businesses may have a difficult time funding their activities. In the U.S., women who are expanding businesses are often perceived as more sophisticated and able to meet their needs on their own. Intermediaries may have difficulty justifying their budgets and their commitment of resources to working with this population. Intermediaries with established self-employment programmes may find that funders view the addition of a programme for expanding busineses as a change of mission.

In spite of these perceptions, intermediaries can make a case for serving larger enterprises if they prepare a thorough needs assessment, demonstrating both why women need this assistance and the economic value they can add. Expanding businesses have a greater potential to generate jobs and provide local employment.

Programmes for women who are starting businesses now exist in most OECD countries. A few of these programmes, such as the Women's Enterprise Development Agency in the U.K. and the Secretariat of State for Women's Rights in France, are providing some individual consulting and training to expanding businesses. The Women's Economic Development Corporation (WEDCO) in the U.S. provides management training for expansion businesses (OECD, 1987). Another U.S. programme with extensive history in this area is the American Women's Economic Development Corporation (AWED) in New York City.

WEDCO differentiates between self-employment and business expansion and has different programmes and services to meet client needs. WEDCO provides extensive management consulting to expanding businesses. It consults on market research, review of competition, and development of a more sophisticated business plan that positions the company for private investment. The Women's Enterprise Development Agency in the U.K. provides similar services to women.

WEDCO also operates a Growth Fund which is specifically aimed at financing women-owned businesses that wish to expand. It typically serves businesses over three years old with two to five employees. The Growth Fund, which has assets of $350 000, is a pilot programme to gain experience and information about the different types of funding needed by expanding businesses. To date, it has made three investments averaging $100 000 per business.

WEDCO assumes a different role in the businesses of borrowers from the Growth Fund than in the businesses it assists under its self-employment program. WEDCO takes a seat on the board of directors and actively advises the business on a continuing basis. As a result, the Growth Fund requires a greater and more expensive time commitment by WEDCO. Investments are made only in businesses which WEDCO can adequately serve with existing staff.

FURTHER RESEARCH REQUIRED

Further research and study should be undertaken on: 1) the appropriate distribution of resources between self-employment and business expansion programmes; 2) the need for expansion programmes which serve women exclusively and 3) how best to meet the financial needs of expanding businesses.

The Distribution of Resources

What are the proper goals for women's enterprise creation strategies? Some experts assert that increasing the number of self-employed women is sufficient in and of itself. Others believe that intermediaries should encourage women to maximise the size of their businesses. Which approach is the best economic strategy? Should one be encouraged over the other? There is continuing debate over the best use of development resources. Self-employment is sometimes seen as marginal economic activity. Businesses offering expansion opportunities are assumed to have greater potential economic impact. These are assertions which cannot be proved or disproved today. They will only be resolved if appropriate data is collected on women's businesses. Until this issue is resolved, it will be difficult to allocate resources between self-employment programmes and business expansion programmes for women.

Women only?

Disagreement exists within OECD countries about the most effective strategies to serve women (OECD, 1987). Even where support exists for self-employment programmes designed exclusively for women, there may not be support for business expansion programmes designed to serve only women.

Some development experts argue that women-owned businesses which choose to expand can be guided into existing economic development programmes. Separate women's organisations may not be able provide adequate resources or business contacts, and may even detract from the status of business women.

Other development experts argue that as long as women face barriers unique to women, separate organisations will better meet their needs. They agree that the private sector can provide management and financial consultants. The issue is whether these consultants are accessible to women's businesses. The answer lies in an assessment of local needs and resources.

In choosing to serve only women, an organisation must focus on women's unique needs today. It must be alert for those changes which occur as women grow and become more sophisticated in business development. Intermediaries must be prepared to grow and change along with their clients. At some point, intermediaries become unnecessary. It is not known exactly when women business owners no longer need special assistance. This is a question which requires further research.

Improving Access to Capital

A third question needing research is how to increase women's access to capital, given that women commonly believe this to be the greatest barrier to business expansion. There needs to be further research on how to eliminate capital gaps. New investment models need to be created and women should be encouraged to invest in each other's firms. Intermediaries should encourage experimentation, develop their own models, and work to redirect existing financial resources. More thoughtful research and evaluation is needed to understand better what capital-related problems are unique to women.

CONCLUSION

The interest in programmes which assist women to expand businesses is very recent. It is an outgrowth of both the success of self-employment programmes and the recognition that barriers do not necessarily fall away simply because women have established successful self-employment businesses. Expansion-oriented programmes may be useful both to complement the growing number of self-employment programmes and to serve women already in business or who have inherited businesses. Until there is more research on women's businesses, and until more programmes serve expanding businesses, it will be difficult to judge the potential contribution of these programmes to local economies.

REFERENCES

Goffee, Robert and Richard Scase (1987) "Patterns of Female Entrepreneurship in Britain", OECD, Paris, p. 11.

Nelton, Sharon (1987) "Polishing Women Entrepreneur", *Nations Business*, July, p. 61.

OECD (1987) "Women, Local Initiatives, Job Creation", Issues Paper, Second International Seminar, April.

Stevenson, Lois (1986) "Against All Odds: The Entrepreneurship of Women", *Journal of Small Business Management*, Vol. 24 (October), p. 35.

Therrien, Lois (1986) "What do Women Want? A Company They Can Call Their Own", *Business Week*, 22 December, p. 61.

Walker, Erika (1988) "Women and Risktaking", *WEDCO EDGE*, Vol.2 no.2, Winter, p. 1.

WEDCO Business Clinic, Client Comments, 1988.

Chapter VI

CONCLUSIONS, RECOMMENDATIONS AND A FRAMEWORK FOR ACTION

Sara Gould and Julia Parzen

INTRODUCTION

We have seen that there are a growing number of effective programmes supporting women's self-employment efforts in the OECD countries. There are also a variety of steps which could be taken to strengthen women's role as entrepreneurs. This final chapter summarises the conclusions of the book concerning women, entrepreneurship and economic development. It also presents a series of recommendations for enhancing the economic contribution of women business owners and suggests a framework for action by each of the partners in the economic development process.

The next section presents the arguments for enterprise creation programmes targeted to women and the lessons which can be drawn from existing pilot programmes. The conclusions reflect the views presented at the Paris and Oslo conferences on women, local employment initiatives and job creation co-sponsored by OECD.

The recommendations address the need for both general human resource development policies (which are of fundamental importance in local economic development) and specific enterprise creation policies. Creating human resource policies which enhance educational opportunity, labour market equality, social support systems and job creation will enable the OECD countries to take full advantage of the expanded participation of women in the labour market. Specific entrepreneurship strategies, including targeting resources to women entrepreneurs and collecting data on women's businesses, will assist the OECD countries specifically to release the entrepreneurial potential of their female citizens. This combination of policies will free women to achieve their full potential, and thereby enhance the resilience and growth of OECD Member country economies.

Successful implementation of these recommendations requires co-operation and co-ordination among a variety of public- and private-sector actors. Every kind of organisation and individual has a part to play. The discussion of the framework for action describes the resources of the key actors and suggests appropriate actions for each in the process of implementing the proposed recommendations.

The chapter ends with a set of guidelines for forming programmes at the local level. Because successful enterprise creation programmes build on the resources and needs at the community level, many such programmes are local initiatives. The guidelines for designing programmes are directed at local activists.

CONCLUSIONS

Encouraging Enterprise Creation is Good Development Policy

Fostering enterprise creation can be an effective economic development strategy. Small and new businesses are an important, and growing, source of jobs and technological innovation. Enterprise creation can also enhance the resilience of local economies and provide new opportunities for disadvantaged groups to participate in, and benefit from, economic growth.

To achieve these goals, enterprise creation strategies must be well focused. Policymakers must be explicit about the kinds of ventures to be encouraged and the goals to be accomplished. Enterprise creation programmes must also fit into an overall development strategy which addresses the competitiveness of traditional industries, promotion of growth industries, appropriate education and training, and improvement of physical infrastructure and services.

Supporting women who want to become entrepreneurs can greatly expand the pool of entrepreneurs in a community and thereby improve the potential for success of any new enterprise development strategy.

Women's Economic Contribution Deserves the Attention of Policymakers

Women are important economic players whose labour force participation, employment and earnings are growing rapidly. Women's economic activities make a substantial contribution to economic growth. Their incomes sustain many families. No market economy can thrive unless it utilises its best human resources. The best person for a job may be a man, or she may be a woman.

Nevertheless, women face disadvantages in several areas which keep them from achieving their full economic potential. Girls are still not encouraged — and, in some cases, are not given equal opportunity — to pursue non-traditional subjects of study or training which could broaden their career choices. Occupational segregation persists because of unequal access to training, continued sex discrimination in hiring practices, and historical social norms and traditions. For similar reasons, women's earnings continue to be lower than men's. In addition, while many women want, or need, to work full-time, they are not always allowed to do so. In most OECD countries, women still bear all of the family responsibilities. They can not even turn to child and parent care services because these are not available at a reasonable cost.

Labour market, social, and education and training policies which eliminate the inequities women face in labour markets will enhance the productive contribution of women to the OECD countries. These steps will also allow more women to become successful entrepreneurs.

Enterprise Creation Programmes Should Target Women

Women business owners are active and visible in the local economies of all 24 OECD countries. The growth in the number of women-owned businesses is expected to continue, spurred on by women's high labour force participation, persistent occupational segregation which limits employment opportunities, and inflexible working hours coupled with inadequate child care options. Other factors which are encouraging women to become self-employed include the greater public-sector encouragement of women-owned businesses, the growing acceptance of women as business owners due to their increasing numbers and the economic impact of their businesses, and the interest of women themselves in entrepreneurship.

While the growth in women's business ownership is encouraging, the size of most women's businesses is small in terms of both turnover and number of employees. And, in all OECD countries, the majority of women's businesses are concentrated in a few sectors, reflecting their owners' previous employment experience.

Women Face Unique Barriers to Business Ownership

Women pursuing business ownership face barriers related to their status in society, their lack of access to information and technical expertise, and their lack of access to capital. While the visibility of women business owners has never been higher, their credibility in the eyes of the general public in this relatively new role remains low. The assumption that a woman's work in the paid labour market is secondary to her homemaking and child-rearing responsibilities prevails in most OECD countries. The lack of supportive public policy in areas like child and dependent care reflects these attitudes, and poses formidable barriers to women starting businesses.

While all new business owners have trouble locating reliable sources of information and technical assistance, this task is particularly difficult for women. Providers of training and technical assistance often dismiss women's business activities as "hobbies", and generally fail to design programme techniques that take into account women's experience and needs. In addition, a great deal of information about such key business topics as quality suppliers, new market opportunities and potential contacts travels person-to-person through informal networks from which women are frequently excluded.

Women's lack of credibility as business owners is nowhere more evident than in the credit arena. Whether she seeks financing from her spouse, another family member or friend, or a conventional lender, women are likely to encounter the assumption that they cannot manage money successfully, particularly in a business context. In addition, the type and relatively small scale of many women's businesses pose barriers in meeting the minimum loan size and collateral requirements characteristic of conventional lenders.

All women encounter these obstacles, yet they are not equally affected by them. A middle class college-educated woman with savings, pertinent management experience, and a supportive spouse may achieve business ownership easily with no outside assistance. At the same time, for certain groups of women, and women who seek to own certain kinds of businesses, these barriers are magnified many times. For example, women starting businesses in non-traditional sectors can have difficulties in gaining access to informal sources of information. Low-income women and minority women may encounter negative attitudes regarding their ability to do business which are rooted in race and class discrimination. It is important to recognise that women are not a homogeneous group.

Intermediaries Can Assist Women to Overcome Barriers

In a growing number of OECD countries, private and public sector resources are being joined together to create new intermediary organisations — or programmes within existing organisations — to assist women with business start-up and expansion. While all of these efforts are very new, early results indicate that they are effectively assisting women to gain business information, skills, credit and credibility. These intermediaries are building track records which will allow the field to continue to attract both the clients and the financial and human resources necessary for programme success and sustainability.

Intermediary organisations and programmes most often aim to achieve one or more of the following goals:

1. Increasing the number of jobs available at income levels that enable women to support themselves and their families;
2. Increasing business ownership by women;
3. Empowering women through the creation of challenging and satisfying work and increased participation in workplace decision-making; and
4. Broadening the employment and income-generating options available to unemployed and underemployed women. The appropriate set of goals for any locality is revealed only as project organisers undertake a needs assessment.

Needs Assessment is the First Step in Designing Effective Programmes

No two communities are exactly alike with regard to 1) the number, circumstances and experiences of women engaged in or pursuing business ownership, 2) available business-related services, and their responsiveness to meeting women's articulated needs, or 3) the presence of the human and financial resources necessary to design and support new programme initiatives. One community may have many established women business owners willing to participate in a structured mentoring programme to assist less experienced women, while another lacks such role models. In some communities, women may prefer greater access to existing service providers, while in others women want to own and operate a new women-focused organisation. And, of course, the level of human and financial resources available will affect greatly the nature and scope of programme responses.

Given these differences, a thorough needs assessment process is the key to collecting the quantitative and anecdotal information necessary for effective programme design.

To Realise their Full Potential, Women Business Owners must be taken Seriously

Nothing will assist women with business ownership more than taking them seriously. To design effective training, technical assistance or financing services, providers must take seriously women's aspirations and believe in women's ability to realise their dreams.

One way to fulfil this requirement is to establish intermediary organisations or programmes operated by women and designed to serve women only. Many countries have adopted this approach to ensuring that programme design is tailored to women's specific needs. Organisations formed to serve entrepreneurial women have other benefits. They bring visibility to the area of women's business ownership, and often incorporate advocacy into what would otherwise be a strictly service perspective.

However, women-only programmes are not appropriate everywhere. Some communities have existing service providers who take women seriously, view them as a promising target market, and are able to design effective programmes. Other communities can modify existing programmes better to meet women's specific needs. In this case, resulting changes are likely to increase the programme's usefulness for both men and women. Finally, many communities simply do not have a resource base capable of sustaining a women-only organisation.

Programmes for women only are clearly not appropriate if the women they would serve feel that establishing a separate organisation will cut them off from mainstream providers, or if they prefer to approach existing services. In some cases, it may be appropriate for a women-focused programme to be offered by an existing service provider only for a limited period of time, after which women clients are directed into on-going programmes.

No single approach is right everywhere. The culture of a particular country, or community within a country, must be taken into account in determining which approach can most effectively accomplish the desired outcomes.

Effective Training and Technical Assistance Programmes are Client-motivated and Self-paced

Effective training and technical assistance programmes assist women clients to accomplish a set of concrete tasks that lead to successful business start-up and expansion. With regard to start-up, these include developing a business plan, learning business-related language, sharpening decision-making skills, and learning systems, such as recordkeeping, that are crucial to setting up business operations. In the case of expansion, acquiring the management-related skills necessary to operate a larger business is the key task.

The experience of a growing number of programmes indicates that relying on the client's own motivation to start-up or expand is the best mechanism to screen for those women most likely to succeed. Staff skilled in specific technical areas work with clients to accomplish specific tasks within a client-motivated, client-paced framework. Often "homework" is assigned. By failing to complete a homework assignment, a client takes herself out of active participation in the programme. Those who complete assignments on a schedule that they establish make measured, regular progress toward their goal.

Informal Networking Opportunities open up Resources for Women

New business owners often find that other people in similar and complementary businesses are the most valuable source of information about the things that really make a business work — reliable suppliers, new customers and effective ways to reach those customers. They make contact with such people in informal ways, including business lunches with associates, participation in activities organised by a Chamber of Commerce or local business association, and social gatherings in the community.

Because women business owners often experience resistance in gaining entry to traditional, male-dominated networks, women in communities in every OECD country are establishing their own networks for exchanging information, getting support and moving their concerns into the public eye. While these new groups bolster women's confidence and provide networking opportunities, women do not want to be cut off from the established and mainstream business community. As the number of women business owners grows, their acceptance into this community and into formerly all-male clubs and associations may become easier.

Financing for Women's Enterprises is a Missing Link

Capital can not turn a weak business idea into a strong business, but lack of capital can derail a good business idea. Lack of access to start up and small business financing is not unique to women, yet it poses a greater obstacle to their business development efforts.

In general, new companies attempting to raise long-term debt or equity do not have access to formal capital markets. Personal savings account for the majority of capital in most start-up businesses. Growing venture capital sectors in many OECD countries are improving the availability of equity capital, but only for those ventures with a good chance of being sold on public equity markets. Similarly, only very large, well-established companies are able to issue long-term debt in the public debt markets. The crucial capital gap, then, is small amounts of equity and debt with flexible payment terms to finance start-ups and early stage expansions. Women are affected by this capital gap to a greater extent than men. Women have more limited access than men to personal savings and to investments by family, friends, and business associates. In cases where bank loans are available to small businesses, women are less able to obtain them because they have fewer personal assets or business assets — since many own service businesses — as collateral for loans.

Without special financing programmes for women's ventures — or broader programmes which affirmatively seek to serve women — only women who have savings or friends with savings can become entrepreneurs.

The design of any venture financing mechanism should be tailored to participants' backgrounds, types of businesses to be financed, and their stage of development. Models now being experimented with range from free-standing venture funds to loan guarantee programmes operated through banks to group programmes in which a small group of women receive individual loans based upon the group's continued clean credit record.

Business Subsidies are usually not Cost-effective

Programmes to support enterprise creation by women should aim to remove barriers without creating new dependencies. For women to achieve their full economic potential, they need equal opportunities to become successful business owners, i.e. to form businesses which are self-sufficient. To the extent that venture programmes assist women to create businesses which are dependent on operating subsidies, they marginalise women's activities in yet another way.

While women starting businesses may need capital from enterprise development programmes, they should pay the full cost of providing that capital. Programmes can succeed at targeting women who truly need financing only by providing capital at the market rate. Charging market rates of interest ensures that programme funds do not simply substitute for other sources of capital to which a women might have access. This approach is consistent with the experience of older enterprise creation programmes that viable businesses need greater access to capital, not subsidised capital.

Charging market rates of interest also contributes to the effective use of capital pools. Interest income earned by the pools increases their sustainability, and allows them to finance the greatest number of businesses. Charging market rates reinforces a borrower's perception that her loan is a serious obligation, and demonstrates the viability of such investments to other financial institutions.

In a few cases, women need small capital or operating subsidies during the start-up phase which enable their businesses to reach self-sufficiency. These may be the case in depressed communities and regions where start-up costs are above average. In these situations, subsidies may be justifiable. Of course, they are also justified if it is traditional to provide special subsidies to existing companies. New businesses should not be put at a disadvantage. For example, many OECD countries routinely subsidise older manufacturing industries, such as ship-building or steel. New income-producing and job-creating businesses merit the same treatment.

Public and private subsidies are appropriate to support a range of training activities, consulting assistance and other services to entrepreneurial women who can then start and operate businesses without continuing subsidy. Even these services, however, should not be offered without cost. Charging for these services results in a more serious, business-like environment. At the same time, charging only what people can afford enhances the pool of entrepreneurs able to create viable businesses.

Systematic Monitoring and Evaluation is Crucial to Programme Success

After establishing a set of agreed-upon goals, programme operators can monitor programme progress, evaluate results, and learn what works and what does not. Because programme evaluation takes time away from programme activities and its costs are often not covered by funders, evaluation too often receives inadequate attention by programme operators. However, if the enterprise creation field is to develop and grow, and learn from its own mistakes, rigorous programme evaluation is crucial.

RECOMMENDATIONS: HUMAN RESOURCE POLICIES

Recognise Women as Key Players in the Economic Development Process

For too long, women's participation in the labour market has been considered secondary to that of men. Their potential to contribute to the process of economic growth has been largely ignored. This point of view no longer makes social, political or economic sense. Sustaining growth in the OECD country economies is increasingly dependent on making the best use of all available resources. Women have experience, skills, ideas and motivation. Communities, regions and countries that continue to ignore these vital resources do so at the peril of sacrificing economic prosperity.

The OECD countries can demonstrate their recognition of women as an economic force by designing educational, social and industrial policies which address the needs of women in the labour market. Government departments with purview over women's issues need to focus on how women can be assisted to meet their full economic potential. All government departments should examine their role in enabling women to achieve economic equality. Many so-called "women's issues", including availablity of child care and health insurance at a reasonable cost, are, in fact, economic development issues.

Invest in Human Capital

Economic development is a people-centered process, which means that the entrepreneur herself is the most important input in new business creation. Like men, women cannot achieve their full potential unless they have access to a range of educational and training options and opportunities.

This investment in human capital must start early. If teachers and administrators expect as much from girls as boys, they will get it. All school curricula through post-secondary levels should require mathematics, science, and economics classes. Academic advisers should track students based on ability rather than gender. Career advisers should offer the same options, including higher education, to all students. No courses should be offered to girls only (such as home economics) or to boys only (such as carpentry). Girls should be encouraged to participate in co-educational team activities. Vocational schools should actively recruit young women. Boys and girls should be

91

actively exposed to role models of women pursuing non-traditional occupations and lifestyles. "Allowing" girls to pursue a non-traditional path is not enough. To overcome a lifetime of socialisation, girls must be encouraged and rewarded for pursuing non-traditional paths.

Women who have already completed their education, however, will not benefit from these changes in opportunity. Given the low pay and uncertain employment prospects for women in traditionally female jobs, developing educational programmes aimed at older women is key. Women already in the labour market will advance only if they can develop new skills and management capability. Occupational training courses should actively recruit women.

Pursue Equality in Labour Markets

Despite recent gains made by women in the labour market, they continue to receive lower pay than men for work of comparable value and to work in a small number of female-dominated occupations. Reducing the extent of occupational segregation is a key way that policymakers can improve women's employment prospects and conditions in the long run. While labour market policies alone cannot accomplish this goal, they play an important role. The vigorous enforcement of anti-discriminatory employment policies will also assist in increasing the number of women in traditionally male jobs. Because high employment growth is projected in traditionally female occupations, comparable worth legislation may also be necessary to eliminate the pay gap.

Implement Social Policies which Recognise Economic Realities

As long as women must juggle household and workplace responsibilities because affordable child care options are scarce, change in their labour market status will come slowly. Family and social policy reforms are necessary. Policy intiatives, such as state-supported child care, parental leave and the provision of full or proportional health and welfare benefits to part-time workers will improve the status of working women.

Design new Industrial Policies

Industrial policies have traditionally benefited established manufacturing industries and the largest firms in those industries. However, the majority of new jobs (and most new jobs for women) are being created in the service sector, and at least as many jobs are being created by small firms as large ones. Policymakers attempting to enhance job creation must first understand these sectoral shifts and analyse their effect on productivity, wages, job quality and the ways in which technology is used and disseminated. With this information, they can develop industrial policies aimed at producing the greatest number of high quality jobs.

At least some of the new industrial policies are likely to target new and small businesses. As a result, while traditional industrial policies have had a national perspective, the new industrial policies will have to take into account regional differences in economic base, markets, management expertise and experience. These local differences determine the kinds of enterprise creation strategies that will be effective.

RECOMMENDATIONS: SPECIFIC ENTERPRISE CREATION POLICIES

Collect More and Better Data on Women's Business Ownership

Currently, most of the OECD countries collect only limited information on women's business ownership. Most countries which collect data on small businesses do not disaggregate it by sex. As a result, researchers have been unable to explain fully why certain characteristics of women's businesses differ from the norm. The absence of this data masks a full understanding of the problems unique to women's businesses and diverts attention from finding solutions to these problems.

Developing innovative policy initiatives requires more and better quality information. A better data base would enable researchers to examine the changes in women's businesses over time and their role in promoting economic development. It would increase awareness of the economic contribution made by women entrepreneurs, and identify ways that women's businesses development efforts could be bolstered by public policy.

It would also be helpful if the OECD countries used uniform classifications of businesses when collecting data on women-owned firms. Currently, each country aggregates data in a different way, making it difficult to compare data across countries.

Case studies on successful women entrepreneurs and their businesses would provide valuable insights into the factors that led to success and the forms of support that might assist other women. Such studies also would highlight and analyse the experience of female role models to encourage other women to pursue self-employment. Diverse role models are needed of women of various ages, income levels, background, ethnic groups, type of business and scale of business activity.

Finally, on-going and comprehensive evaluations of current entrepreneurship programmes in the OECD countries would reveal whether they have promoted venture creation, how they could more effectively accomplish their goals, and which are the best models. With the performance data now available, it is difficult to draw out the lessons learned or to judge whether most programmes have been a success.

Develop and Promote New Images of Women Business Owners

The development of positive and visible role models is crucial to increasing the total number of women business owners. Any woman who starts up a business is embarking on a non-traditional path. Knowing that other women have travelled that path before her builds self-esteem and inspires the courage necessary to realise her aspirations.

As new images are developed, it is important that they highlight many different kinds of women owning many different kinds of businesses. Women of all races and ethnicities, young women, older women, single women with children, married women, rich women, low-income women, can all be business owners.

To reach the public eye, new images of women business owners should be featured in educational campaigns carried out through traditional institutions and in the media. Children in elementary, middle and secondary schools, as well as guidance and career counsellors, should have the opportunity to meet and talk with women in business. Attention in the mainstream media can recognise individual achievement, while bringing greater visibility for all women business owners.

Support Model Programmes to Learn What Works and What Does Not

Newly-created intermediary organisations and programmes are experimenting with a variety of approaches to meet women's training, credit and personal needs in relation to self-employment and business expansion. This experimentation will yield valuable lessons about what works and what does not. It is essential to designing more effective business development services for women and men.

To continue to develop, intermediaries need support of various kinds. Adequate levels of funding must be gathered from both public- and private-sector donors to meet programme operating costs and to capitalise loan funds and other financing mechanisms. In addition, mainstream practitioners can make a significant difference in the progress of new intermediaries by lending their expertise, legitimacy and credibility. Finally, policy-makers can contribute by designing creative solutions to institutional and systemic barriers which are identified through local operation.

Target Resources to Meet Local needs and to Promote Non-traditional Enterprises and Entrepreneurs

To achieve the greatest impact, public and private institutions in any locality or region should target their resources to support priority activities identified through a thorough needs assessment process. In one area, such a process might reveal a gap in seed capital available for women's businesses, while in another it might identify five women's businesses that are prime for expansion. In yet another, the pressing need may be to extend the option of self-employment into low-income and minority communities. Whatever the priorities identified, available resources will be spent more effectively and efficiently if they are targeted to meet them.

At the same time, there are two areas which clearly merit resources in all OECD countries. Resources should be targeted to increase the number of women-owned businesses operating in non-traditional sectors and to broaden the economic options available to low-income women.

Throughout all OECD countries, women-owned businesses are under-represented in many sectors, including manufacturing, construction, mining, transportation, communications and finance. This is a key factor in explaining the income gap faced by women in relation to their male counterparts. Within any sector, this income gap may be partially explained by the young age of many women-owned businesses. Overall, however, it is explained by the heavy concentration of women-owned businesses in low-return, traditionally female, industrial sectors. Targeting of training and financial resources to create opportunities and incentives for women to move into more lucrative sectors is one way to increase the incomes that women derive from business ownership.

The option of self-employment and small business development may have particular merit for low-income women. In every community, women who cannot find a job, or cannot make ends meet with one job, are using various talents to engage in small-scale, home-based, informal business activities. These "entrepreneurs of necessity" or "creative survivors" may not fit the traditional profile of a business owner, and often would not call themselves such, but, in some cases, their marginal activities can be bolstered to create an income on which they can support themselves and their families. While no panacea, self-employment is a viable option for some low-income women.

FRAMEWORK FOR ACTION

The preceding recommendations represent a broad and diverse set of activities that will, over time, lead to the full and productive participation of women in the surge of entrepreneurial activity now occurring in the OECD Member countries. How will these recommendations be implemented? Which actors must participate, and what steps can they take? This framework for action identifies the key actors and discusses their potential contributions.

National, Regional and Local Government

The most important role of the public sector in promoting women and entrepreneurship is to design and implement policies which encourage private citizens and institutions to pursue enterprise creation. The public sector can fulfil this role by 1) adopting overall economic policies which promote small business development and remove barriers facing women who want to start businesses, and 2) providing grants and subsidies to public/private partnerships in enterprise creation.

There are a variety of public policies which national governments could implement to facilitate small business development. For example, national governments could increase the availability of venture capital by reducing taxes for long-term investments in small businesses. Revising regulations governing the issuance of securities to reduce the registration costs associated with small new issues is another way to make it easier for young companies to raise capital.

Of course, national governments must also take the lead in establishing the labour market, social, and education policies described in the "Recommendations". For example, national health insurance and funding for day care services would free women to create businesses and to spend more time on their existing businesses. National governments also have the power to enforce anti-discrimination legislation and promote affirmative action. They can modify personal income tax and social security systems which penalise two-earner couples. They can eliminate laws which require women to obtain their husband's approval on decisions or bar women from owning assets. They can also promote images of women as equal players in the economic arena, and award public recognition to organisations which do the same.

Both national and local governments can make a valuable contribution to enterprise creation by funding local capacity building, needs assessment and programme creation. Government funds are a critical contribution to the partnership. National and local governments can also design incentives that reward private investors for participating in venture creation in depressed communities.

Actions

— Adopt overall economic policies which promote small business development;
— Adopt labour market, social, and educational policies which remove barriers facing women attempting business start-ups;
— Provide grants and subsidies to public/private partnerships.

Private-sector large corporations, the small business sector, and private non-profit business development organisations each have unique resources which can enhance enterprise creation by women.

Large corporations can play a variety of roles. They can train and promote women managers, serving as a training ground in which women with entrepreneurial talent have the opportunity to learn and practise management skills. Large corporations also subcontract with smaller businesses for products and services. They can create new business opportunities for women-owned firms by making a special effort to contract with them. Corporations also have talented employees who could be loaned (seconded) on a temporary basis to staff a new business support or training organisation. Finally, corporations which have established foundations or corporate giving programmes have another essential resource to contribute: funding to underwrite the costs of a community-based needs assessment process or pilot a new training programme targeted to women interested in business ownership.

The small business sector has several different kinds of resources. Perhaps the most important of these is the small business person herself or himself. People already in business represent a wealth of information, expertise, ideas and networking contacts for women just starting out. In some cases, they may have the skills and the time to be active and effective mentors to women new to business ownership.

Private, non-profit business support organisations make training, technical assistance and, often financing programmes accessible to people pursuing business start-up or expansion. If such organisations take women clients seriously and design their programmes to meet the special barriers that women face, they can be active participants in any community effort to bring more women into business ownership.

Actions

— Promote women to top management levels in large corporations;
— Fund training programmes for women;
— Serve as mentors, advisors and contacts for women starting or expanding small businesses;
— Provide training, technical assistance and financing programmes designed to meet the needs of women.

Women's Organisations

Women's organisations take many different forms and pursue a range of activities. Service organisations — such as women's employment programmes, women's centres, and shelters for battered women — provide short and long-term training and self-help services to a variety of women clients. Associations of women business owners offer opportunities for their members to network with each other, as well as with more established business owners and mainstream business development resources.

In the process of increasing the support available to women pursuing business ownership, women's organisations bring the most valuable resources — concern for, connections to, in-depth knowledge about, and understanding of women themselves. Organisations with a women's perspective can draw attention to the issue of women's business ownership, express and share the experience of women attempting business ownership, and advocate for the resources necessary to bolster women's efforts.

In addition, they bring expertise in such areas as designing effective training techniques for use with different kinds of women, building women's self-confidence and self-esteem, and meeting women's needs for child and dependent care, transportation and other key support services. Their work with, and advocacy on behalf of, women ensures that women's concerns will continue to be heard and taken into account.

Actions

— Raise the issue of women's business ownership within a community or region;
— Bring together representatives from business, education, service, labour and other sectors to participate in a needs assessment process;

— Provide expertise in the process of designing new programmes and services to meet women's articulated needs;

— Monitor and publicize the results of new efforts to expand women's business ownership.

Financial Institutions

Financial institutions can become partners with successful venture creation programmes. In effective partnerships, venture programmes take on the tasks of screening and preparing applicants and providing technical assistance to loan recipients. In return, financial institutions agree to consider seriously loans to applicants that they may have otherwise deemed too risky or time-consuming. Financial institutions can also contribute operating support to intermediaries. In the long run, this kind of partnership benefits the financial institution by identifying new loan customers.

Financial institutions can make sure that the loan application process is clear and easy to understand. Bank lending criteria frequently are not spelled out, and women are likely to be unfamiliar with the lending process. Bankers can make a difference by being prepared to explain their loan process to intermediaries working with women (as well as to individual loan applicants), and making sure applicants know what to include in their application and how to present the information.

Financial institutions can train and encourage staff to treat women loan applicants in the same way as men. This requires several steps. First, financial institutions must change the attitudes of lending officers toward women. Women should be treated as potentially valuable customers. Second, financial institutions must familiarise themselves with the financing needs of service businesses. The service sector accounts for the vast majority of women's businesses, and financial institutions can benefit by developing appropriate loan products. Third, financial institutions must familiarise themselves with, and aggressively use, public and private programmes which limit loan losses or lower lending costs.

Actions

— Become partners with intermediary programmes;

— Make lending requirements simple and clear;

— Treat women loan applicants in the same way as men.

Other Non-profit Partners

Trade unions play different roles in the various OECD countries which determine what their contribution to the women's venture partnership should be. Trade unions are a source of important data and statistical research on the changing patterns of women's employment. They can also offer training and apprenticeships to women in non-traditional fields and recruit more women to be union members. Educational institutions are the primary vehicle for implementing the education recommendations described earlier. Without access to increased educational opportunity, diverse new role models early in life, and encouragement to experiment with a variety of employment options, women's advancement in the labour market will be limited.

Business associations are an important, often informal, means whereby new and expanding businesses find suppliers, employees and customers. Women's access to this resource has been limited, in part because business associations often harbour negative attitudes toward women in business. Business associations can participate in the partnership by encouraging membership by women and facilitating their involvement.

Trade Union Actions

— Collect data on women's employment patterns;
— Offer training and apprenticeships to women in non-traditional fields.

Educational Institution Actions

— Provide equal educational access;
— Encourage new role models.

Business Association Actions

— Encourage participation by women;
— Where necessary, establish special programmes for women.

GUIDELINES FOR FORMING PROGRAMMES AT THE LOCAL LEVEL

Having identified the people and institutions that need to be involved, the task remains to motivate them and organise their actions into a co-ordinated and strategic plan. Who should take on this responsibility? What needs to be accomplished?

Several different organisations, acting alone or in coalition, can take on the leadership role in forming a new intermediary. A women business owner organisation, a local department of community or economic development, a commission on the status of women, a women's advocacy organisation or chamber of commerce are all logical leaders. In its *Working Guide to Women's Self-Employment*, the National Coalition for Women's Enterprise in the U.S. suggests that the following types of capacity are needed in any group, or coalition of groups, that take on leadership:

— A commitment to participation in an inclusive and responsive process and an established track record in programme implementation, especially in such areas as public relations and marketing;
— Ability to reach both women business owners and women with an active interest in self-employment, and to motivate them to participate in the process. This ability must extend across traditional economic, ethnic/racial and age boundaries;
— Knowledge of the business development and economic development processes;
— Established working relationships, or the ability to establish such relationships, with individuals in leadership positions within the local economic development, government, business, financial, educational, and neighbourhood development arenas, and within the minority and women's business communities;
— Ability to attract financial resources;
— Willingness to commit substantial time (Gould and Lyman, 1987, p. 110).

As discussed in chapter IV, the first step in designing a co-ordinated plan is assessing the community's needs and resources. This process involves guaging the interest in enterprise development among women in the community, exploring their experiences with business ownership and identifying barriers and opportunities, and learning about the community's existing business development support services. With this information, leaders can identify gaps in existing local service delivery to women and design an initial set of responsive local programme and policy initiatives.

Chapters III, IV and V describe local, regional and national programmes and policies aimed at supporting the entrepreneurial efforts of women. The rich diversity and variety of these responses illustrates well the decisions that local and national planners and policymakers face in formulating a set of responses that will be effective in any given area. These decisions include:

— Should we create a new organisation, or add services to an existing one?
— Should we design women-only services? If we begin with women-only programmes, should women clients be integrated into mainstream programmes over time?
— What set of services will respond to the barriers faced by women and create new opportunities for women?
— What resources — time, money, skills — can we attract?

The answers to these questions will vary widely from place to place and circumstance to circumstance.

In all cases, however, collaboration and partnership are essential in the process of finding the answers to the above questions. The chances for effective and innovative programme design will be enhanced if all of the available skills and resources within a community are brought to bear. The framework for action outlined earlier in this chapter discusses the range of actors and suggests specific actions that each can take as they become involved in local and national programme and policy design. Chapters I and II present compelling arguments which programme developers can use to motivate these actors and secure their participation. It is only through partnership that the goals of promoting women, entrepreneurship and economic development will be accomplished.

REFERENCES

Gould, Sara K. and Jing Lyman (1987) *A Working Guide to Women's Self-Employment*, Corporation for Enterprise Development, February. Prepared under a grant from the Economic Development Administration of the U.S. Department of Commerce.

MAIN SALES OUTLETS OF OECD PUBLICATIONS – PRINCIPAUX POINTS DE VENTE DES PUBLICATIONS DE L'OCDE

Argentina – Argentine
Carlos Hirsch S.R.L.
Galería Güemes, Florida 165, 4° Piso
1333 Buenos Aires   Tel. (1) 331.1787 y 331.2391
Telefax: (1) 331.1787

Australia – Australie
D.A. Book (Aust.) Pty. Ltd.
648 Whitehorse Road, P.O.B 163
Mitcham, Victoria 3132   Tel. (03) 873.4411
Telefax: (03) 873.5679

Austria – Autriche
OECD Publications and Information Centre
Schedestrasse 7
D-W 5300 Bonn 1 (Germany)   Tel. (49.228) 21.60.45
Telefax: (49.228) 26.11.04

Gerold & Co.
Graben 31
Wien I   Tel. (0222) 533.50.14

Belgium – Belgique
Jean De Lannoy
Avenue du Roi 202
B-1060 Bruxelles   Tel. (02) 538.51.69/538.08.41
Telefax: (02) 538.08.41

Canada
Renouf Publishing Company Ltd.
1294 Algoma Road
Ottawa, ON K1B 3W8   Tel. (613) 741.4333
Telefax: (613) 741.5439

Stores:
61 Sparks Street
Ottawa, ON K1P 5R1   Tel. (613) 238.8985
211 Yonge Street
Toronto, ON M5B 1M4   Tel. (416) 363.3171

Federal Publications
165 University Avenue
Toronto, ON M5H 3B8   Tel. (416) 581.1552
Telefax: (416)581.1743

Les Éditions La Liberté Inc.
3020 Chemin Sainte-Foy
Sainte-Foy, PQ G1X 3V6   Tel. (418) 658.3763
Telefax: (418) 658.3763

China – Chine
China National Publications Import
Export Corporation (CNPIEC)
P.O. Box 88
Beijing   Tel. 44.0731
Telefax: 401.5661

Denmark – Danemark
Munksgaard Export and Subscription Service
35, Nørre Søgade, P.O. Box 2148
DK-1016 København K   Tel. (33) 12.85.70
Telefax: (33) 12.93.87

Finland – Finlande
Akateeminen Kirjakauppa
Keskuskatu 1, P.O. Box 128
00100 Helsinki   Tel. (358 0) 12141
Telefax: (358 0) 121.4441

France
OECD/OCDE
Mail Orders/Commandes par correspondance:
2, rue André-Pascal
75775 Paris Cédex 16   Tel. (33-1) 45.24.82.00
Telefax: (33-1) 45.24.85.00
or (33-1) 45.24.81.76
Telex: 620 160 OCDE

Bookshop/Librairie:
33, rue Octave-Feuillet
75016 Paris   Tel. (33-1) 45.24.81.67
(33-1) 45.24.81.81

Librairie de l'Université
12a, rue Nazareth
13100 Aix-en-Provence   Tel. 42.26.18.08
Telefax: 42.26.63.26

Germany – Allemagne
OECD Publications and Information Centre
Schedestrasse 7
D-W 5300 Bonn 1   Tel. (0228) 21.60.45
Telefax: (0228) 26.11.04

Greece – Grèce
Librairie Kauffmann
Mavrokordatou 9
106 78 Athens   Tel. 322.21.60
Telefax: 363.39.67

Hong Kong
Swindon Book Co. Ltd.
13 - 15 Lock Road
Kowloon, Hong Kong   Tel. 366.80.31
Telefax: 739.49.75

Iceland – Islande
Mál Mog Menning
Laugavegi 18, Pósthólf 392
121 Reykjavik   Tel. 162.35.23

India – Inde
Oxford Book and Stationery Co.
Scindia House
New Delhi 110001   Tel.(11) 331.5896/5308
Telefax: (11) 332.5993

17 Park Street
Calcutta 700016   Tel. 240832

Indonesia – Indonésie
Pdii-Lipi
P.O. Box 269/JKSMG/88
Jakarta 12790   Tel. 583467
Telex: 62 875

Ireland – Irlande
TDC Publishers – Library Suppliers
12 North Frederick Street
Dublin 1   Tel. 74.48.35/74.96.77
Telefax: 74.84.16

Israel
Elecronic Publications only
Publications électroniques seulement
Sophist Systems Ltd.
71 Allenby Street
Tel-Aviv 65134   Tel. 3-29.00.21
Telefax: 3-29.92.39

Italy – Italie
Libreria Commissionaria Sansoni
Via Duca di Calabria 1/1
50125 Firenze   Tel. (055) 64.54.15
Telefax: (055) 64.12.57

Via Bartolini 29
20155 Milano   Tel. (02) 36.50.83
Editrice e Libreria Herder
Piazza Montecitorio 120
00186 Roma   Tel. 679.46.28
Telex: NATEL I 621427

Libreria Hoepli
Via Hoepli 5
20121 Milano   Tel. (02) 86.54.46
Telefax: (02) 805.28.86

Libreria Scientifica
Dott. Lucio de Biasio 'Aeiou'
Via Meravigli 16
20123 Milano   Tel. (02) 805.68.98
Telefax: (02) 80.01.75

Japan – Japon
OECD Publications and Information Centre
Landic Akasaka Building
2-3-4 Akasaka, Minato-ku
Tokyo 107   Tel. (81.3) 3586.2016
Telefax: (81.3) 3584.7929

Korea – Corée
Kyobo Book Centre Co. Ltd.
P.O. Box 1658, Kwang Hwa Moon
Seoul   Tel. 730.78.91
Telefax: 735.00.30

Malaysia – Malaisie
Co-operative Bookshop Ltd.
University of Malaya
P.O. Box 1127, Jalan Pantai Baru
59700 Kuala Lumpur
Malaysia   Tel. 756.5000/756.5425
Telefax: 757.3661

Netherlands – Pays-Bas
SDU Uitgeverij
Christoffel Plantijnstraat 2
Postbus 20014
2500 EA's-Gravenhage   Tel. (070 3) 78.99.11
Voor bestellingen: Tel. (070 3) 78.98.80
Telefax: (070 3) 47.63.51

New Zealand – Nouvelle-Zélande
GP Publications Ltd.
Customer Services
33 The Esplanade - P.O. Box 38-900
Petone, Wellington   Tel. (04) 5685.555
Telefax: (04) 5685.333

Norway – Norvège
Narvesen Info Center - NIC
Bertrand Narvesens vei 2
P.O. Box 6125 Etterstad
0602 Oslo 6   Tel. (02) 57.33.00
Telefax: (02) 68.19.01

Pakistan
Mirza Book Agency
65 Shahrah Quaid-E-Azam
Lahore 3   Tel. 66.839
Telex: 44886 UBL PK. Attn: MIRZA BK

Portugal
Livraria Portugal
Rua do Carmo 70-74
Apart. 2681
1117 Lisboa Codex   Tel.: (01) 347.49.82/3/4/5
Telefax: (01) 347.02.64

Singapore – Singapour
Information Publications Pte. Ltd.
Pei-Fu Industrial Building
24 New Industrial Road No. 02-06
Singapore 1953   Tel. 283.1786/283.1798
Telefax: 284.8875

Spain – Espagne
Mundi-Prensa Libros S.A.
Castelló 37, Apartado 1223
Madrid 28001   Tel. (91) 431.33.99
Telefax: (91) 575.39.98

Libreria Internacional AEDOS
Consejo de Ciento 391
08009 - Barcelona   Tel. (93) 488.34.92
Telefax: (93) 487.76.59

Llibreria de la Generalitat
Palau Moja
Rambla dels Estudis, 118
08002 - Barcelona   Tel. (93) 318.80.12 (Subscripcions)
(93) 302.67.23 (Publicacions)
Telefax: (93) 412.18.54

Sri Lanka
Centre for Policy Research
c/o Colombo Agencies Ltd.
No. 300-304, Galle Road
Colombo 3   Tel. (1) 574240, 573551-2
Telefax: (1) 575394, 510711

Sweden – Suède
Fritzes Fackboksföretaget
Box 16356
Regeringsgatan 12
103 27 Stockholm   Tel. (08) 23.89.00
Telefax: (08) 20.50.21

Subscription Agency/Abonnements:
Wennergren-Williams AB
Nordenflychtsvägen 74
Box 30004
104 25 Stockholm   Tel. (08) 13.67.00
Telefax: (08) 618.62.32

Switzerland – Suisse
OECD Publications and Information Centre
Schedestrasse 7
D-W 5300 Bonn 1 (Germany)   Tel. (49.228) 21.60.45
Telefax: (49.228) 26.11.04

Suisse romande
Maditec S.A.
Chemin des Palettes 4
1020 Renens/Lausanne   Tel. (021) 635.08.65
Telefax: (021) 635.07.80

Librairie Payot
6 rue Grenus
1211 Genève 11   Tel. (022) 731.89.50
Telex: 28356

Subscription Agency – Service des Abonnements
Naville S.A.
7, rue Lévrier
1201 Genève   Tél.: (022) 732.24.00
Telefax: (022) 738.87.13

Taiwan – Formose
Good Faith Worldwide Int'l. Co. Ltd.
9th Floor, No. 118, Sec. 2
Chung Hsiao E. Road
Taipei   Tel. (02) 391.7396/391.7397
Telefax: (02) 394.9176

Thailand – Thaïlande
Suksit Siam Co. Ltd.
113, 115 Fuang Nakhon Rd.
Opp. Wat Rajbopith
Bangkok 10200   Tel. (662) 251.1630
Telefax: (662) 236.7783

Turkey – Turquie
Kültur Yayinlari Is-Türk Ltd. Sti.
Atatürk Bulvari No. 191/Kat. 21
Kavaklidere/Ankara   Tel. 25.07.60
Dolmabahce Cad. No. 29
Besiktas/Istanbul   Tel. 160.71.88
Telex: 43482B

United Kingdom – Royaume-Uni
HMSO
Gen. enquiries   Tel. (071) 873 0011
Postal orders only:
P.O. Box 276, London SW8 5DT
Personal Callers HMSO Bookshop
49 High Holborn, London WC1V 6HB
Telefax: 071 873 2000
Branches at: Belfast, Birmingham, Bristol, Edinburgh,
Manchester

United States – États-Unis
OECD Publications and Information Centre
2001 L Street N.W., Suite 700
Washington, D.C. 20036-4910   Tel. (202) 785.6323
Telefax: (202) 785.0350

Venezuela
Libreria del Este
Avda F. Miranda 52, Aptdo. 60337
Edificio Galipán
Caracas 106   Tel. 951.1705/951.2307/951.1297
Telegram: Libreste Caracas

Yugoslavia – Yougoslavie
Jugoslovenska Knjiga
Knez Mihajlova 2, P.O. Box 36
Beograd   Tel. (011) 621.992
Telefax: (011) 625.970

Orders and inquiries from countries where Distributors have
not yet been appointed should be sent to: OECD Publications Service, 2 rue André-Pascal, 75775 Paris Cédex 16,
France.

Les commandes provenant de pays où l'OCDE n'a pas
encore désigné de distributeur devraient être adressées à :
OCDE, Service des Publications, 2, rue André-Pascal, 75775
Paris Cédex 16, France.

OECD PUBLICATIONS, 2 rue André-Pascal, 75775 PARIS CEDEX 16
PRINTED IN FRANCE
(84 90 02 1) ISBN 92-64-13436-0 - No. 45385 1990